Rapid Problem Solving with Post-it® Notes

David Straker, MS, is a quality consultant with Hewlett Packard, UK, where he researches, writes, teaches and consults on business methods. His previous experience includes teaching, managing, engineering and marketing. This is his third book.

Rapid Problem Solving with Post-it® Notes

David Straker

FISHER
er
BOOKS.™

For Eleri

While Honey lies in Every Flower, no doubt,
It takes a Bee to get the Honey out.

Arthur Guiterman, *A Poet's Proverbs*, 1924

Publishers: Bill Fisher
          Helen V. Fisher
          Howard W. Fisher
North American editor: Melanie Mallon
Managing editor: Sarah Trotta
Book production: Deanie Wood
             Randy Schultz
Cartoons: Simon Kitson
Cover design: Gary Smith,
          Performance Design

First published in Great Britain in 1997
by Gower Publishing Limited,
Aldershot, Hampshire

North American edition published by
Fisher Books
4239 W. Ina Road, Suite 101
Tucson, Arizona 85741
(520) 744-6110

Library of Congress Cataloging-in-Publication Data

Straker, David.
Rapid problem-solving with Post-it Notes
/ David Straker. - - North American ed.
     p.   cm.
   Includes index.
   ISBN 1-55561-142-7
   1. Sticky notes. 2. Paperwork (Office
practice) - -Management. 3. Problem
solving.   I. Title.
HF5547. 15.S77 1997
651.7'4- -dc21   96-20721
                  CIP

Printed in U.S.A.
10 9 8 7 6 5 4 3 2 1

Contents

Acknowledgments

Books are seldom written by a single person in isolation, and this one is no exception. I have had much help from many friends and family along the way, so this is a big thank you to at least:

At HP: For encouragement and suggestions, Peter Auber, Simon Bedford-Roberts, David Gee, John Hamilton, Philip Nield, Doug O'Hanlon and David Whittall.

At 3M: Carolyn Morris, for support and supplies, plus Spence Silver, Art Fry, and others for the original glue, idea and development of the magical Post-it® Note.

At Gower: Malcolm Stern and Solveig Servian for faith and everything that publishers do.

At his place: Simon Kitson for the splendid cartoons.

At home: Eleri, Heledd, Geraint and Bella for love, patience and much, much more.

And not forgetting: You, for buying the book, plus everyone else who lent a hand, an ear, a thought or other support during writing, review and production. Thank you.

Introduction

Do you ever come across problems that seem to be a mess of issues, disagreement and disconnected pieces of information? Do you go around in circles for hours or days, arguing with co-workers and trying to make sense of it all? If so, you're in good company—many other people face such problems every day. It's a sad fact of the messy world we live and work in that problems don't come in tidy packages that are easy to understand and solve.

So what's the answer? First, realize that problems are almost always made up of individual pieces of information that are related to each other in some way. The size of the problem is simply determined by the number of information pieces and the number and type of relationships *among* these pieces. Whether your problem is to build a house, analyze competitive strategy or plan a meal, all you need to know is what the pieces are and how they may be organized to help you understand the problem and produce an effective solution.

Never fear—help is at hand! Armed with this book and a pad of Post-it® Notes, you can bring order to the chaos, coaxing the pieces of your jigsaw puzzle into place.

How can Post-it® Notes help?

Post-it® Notes have three key properties that we can use to help solve these difficult problems:

- They're about the right size to hold one piece of information from a problem.
- They're easy to attach to a smooth surface and they stay where they're put.
- They can be quickly and easily detached and reattached many times.

These properties make Post-it® Notes an ideal basic tool for use in rapid problem-solving. The missing factor, however, is the method. *How* do you get all the right pieces of information? *How* do you organize them to help solve your problem?

That is where this book comes in. It describes a set of tools that are quick and easy to learn and use. You can get to the heart of your problem rapidly and easily. Complex tools are fine for specialists, but most working people don't have the time or energy for sophisticated analytical techniques.

Simple names are used for simple tools. Impressive-sounding names may add to the mystery of specialists, but they're a turn-off for everyone else.

Finally, the tools are described clearly and practically, with many diagrams and examples. The point, after all, is for you to *use* them, not just be impressed by or understand the theory.

3M and Post-it® Notes

In 1968, Spence Silver, a chemist at 3M, was developing adhesives when he came up with a weak, "unsticky" adhesive. There were many attempts to find a use for it in a product. Eventually, an associate named Art Fry, who was also an enthusiastic choir director, discovered a use for the adhesive. One day in 1974, after the bookmarks fell out of his hymnal, he thought about Silver's adhesive. The result was the now-famous Post-it® Notes.

Post-it® Notes didn't become successful right away. In fact they only took off after a steady campaign. In 1978, 3M tried a significant give-away promotion. A large number of those who received the free samples proved the value of the product by coming back for more.

3M owns the brand-name *Post-it®*. They ask that each and every time it's used, the symbol for a registered trademark, ®, be put next to it. They also note that "Post-it®" is an adjective and must be used as such. They produce a wide range of other Post-it® products.

This book was not written by or for 3M, even though it may seem like it. Post-it® Notes are a serious business tool that can be used for rapid problem-solving. Because the registered trademark symbol sprinkled throughout a book can make it hard to read, the word "Note" has been freely used instead. Where you see the word "Note," please read "Post-it® Note."

Tool origins

Most tools are based on previous learning. The Post-it® Note tools described in this book are no different. To a greater or lesser degree, they have been borrowed and adapted from existing problem-solving methods (see table).

Tool	Origins
Post-up	Brainstorming, Brainwriting, Nominal Group Technique, Crawford Slip Method
Swap Sort	Bubble Sort, Paired Comparison, Prioritization Matrix
Top-down Tree	Systematic/Tree Diagram, Cause-Effect Diagram, Why-Why Diagram, How-How Diagram, Process-Decision Program Chart
Bottom-up Tree	Affinity Diagram, KJ Method, Set Theory
Information Map	Relations Diagram, Mind Map, Entity-Relation Diagram, State-Transition Diagram
Action Map	Activity Network, PERT Diagram, Process Flowchart, Data-Flow Diagram

And finally . . .

Only you can make these tools work. If you think this is a great book, but put it on the shelf without using the tools to solve your problems, it will have failed. If, however, you use one tool to help solve one problem, then it will have begun to succeed.

A Quick Tour

Are you impatient to get going? Are you browsing and just want to find out what rapid problem-solving with Post-it® Notes means? Do you use the methods already and just want a quick reminder? If the answer to any of these questions is "yes," then this section is for you.

If you want to start with the background information, how the methods work and the basic details of using them, go to Part I. This section is for people in a hurry who want to see the big picture first, and the detailed parts later.

A Quick Tour

Key principles

Rapid problem-solving with Post-it® Notes uses a few key principles. These principles will help you understand your problem and find the important decision points. Here is a quick summary of these key principles—enough to start you off, but not enough to slow you down on your hurricane tour.

Chunking

- Your mind works by taking in information one individual piece, or *chunk*, at a time. The chunk may be simple, like "a brick," or more complex, such as "my house."
- Information about problems also comes in chunks. It can usually be written in a short phrase or sentence. For example, "The roof is leaking."
- You can capture problem chunks by writing them on Notes.
- You can solve problems by:
  — finding all the chunks
  — arranging them into meaningful patterns
  — focusing on the important parts

Problem patterns

There are three basic ways of arranging chunks:

- *Lists* are simple collections of chunks that may or may not be sorted in order of importance.
- *Trees* have simple hierarchical "parent-and-child" relationships. They can be built top-down or bottom-up.
- *Maps* have more complex relationships. Any chunk is related to any other chunk. They can be used to relate specific actions or general information chunks.

Guiding decisions

- Simple written guidelines help keep sessions on track.
- *Objectives* describe what you're trying to achieve. Non-objectives make clear what you're *not* trying to achieve.
- *Criteria* are the judgment points for making decisions. For example, "must be low-cost."
- *Questions* stimulate and direct thinking.
- *Constraints* limit your choices. For example, "Only John and Jean can use the PR30."

The FOG factor

- An information chunk can be a fact, an opinion or a guess.
- *Facts* can be proven true. They're usually more useful, but are also harder to find or prove.
- *Opinions* are what people believe to be true. They're often mistaken for facts.
- *Guesses* are acknowledged as wild ideas.
- You can write F, O or G on a Note to indicate whether the chunk is a fact, opinion or guess.
- It's often worth taking the time to find information that will change important opinions or guesses into known facts.

Note sessions

- Post-it® Note tools can be used on your own. More often, they're used in meetings with other people who can contribute to solving the problem.
- Guidelines for each tool can be displayed on a separate flipchart where everyone can see them.

The Tools

The Post-up

- The Post-up is the first List tool.
- Use it for collecting information chunks, one per Note.
- In a group, everyone writes chunks and sticks them up at the same time. They do not talk while they're doing this. The result is a focused and efficient information-collection session.

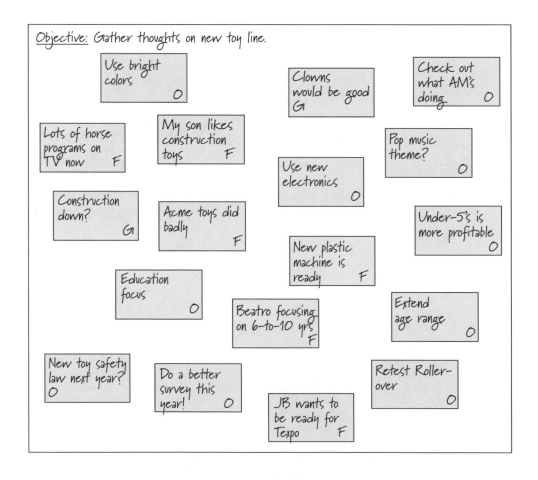

The Swap Sort

- The Swap Sort is the second List tool.
- Use it to sort chunks into an order of importance.
- First reduce the list by combining similar items and rejecting low-priority ones.
- Sort by swapping pairs of Notes, putting the most important one higher up in the list, until no more can be swapped.
- Use the same criterion in each comparison to find the most important Note of each pair.

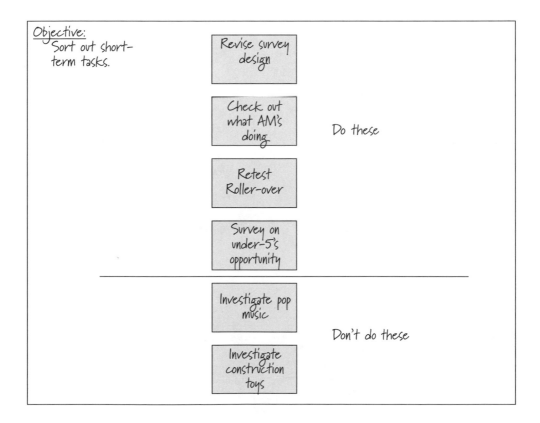

The Top-down Tree

- The Top-down Tree is the first Tree tool.
- Use it to break down a problem when you have little existing information.
- Do this by asking a consistent question about each Note.

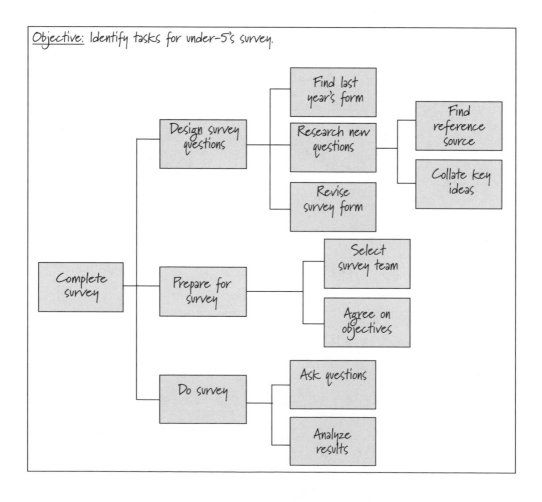

The Bottom-up Tree

- The Bottom-up Tree is the second Tree tool.
- Use it when you have lots of information chunks, but don't understand the fundamental nature of the problem.
- Build up the tree from the bottom by forming groups of Notes. Then group the groups, and so on until there is one "top-level" group.
- Give each group a title to describe what it contains.

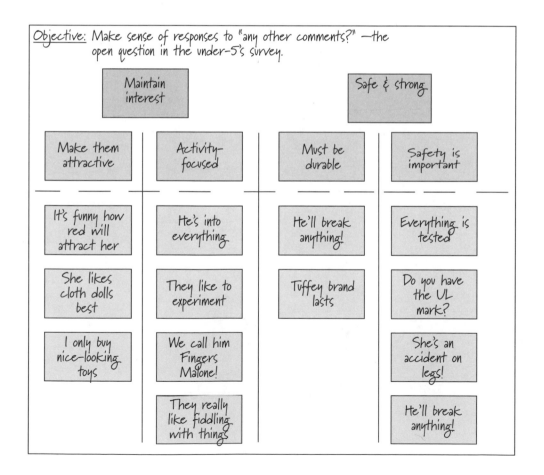

The Information Map

- The Information Map is the first Map tool.
- Use it to map messy problems, where information chunks have complex interrelationships.
- First identify chunks and place related ones near each another. Then show the relationships with arrows.

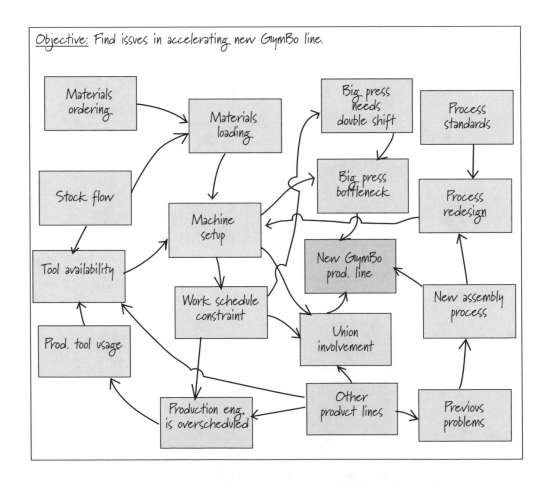

The Action Map

- The Action Map is the second Map tool.
- Use it to plan actions or map an existing process.
- Use one chunk for each action. Then place them in order of action.
- Add arrows to show this order more clearly.

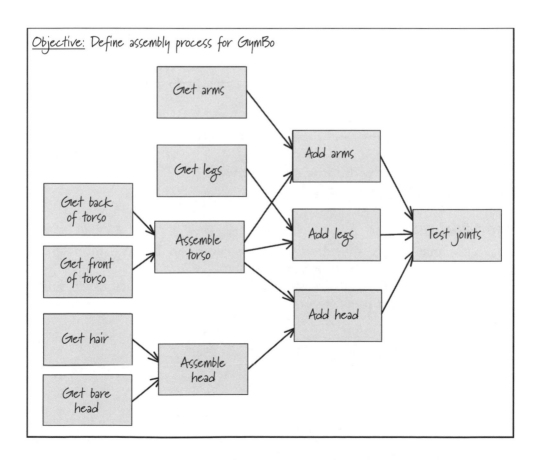

Tools in Practice

The Post-it® Note tools are of little value unless you make practical use of them.

Frameworks

You can make the process of solving problems more predictable and reliable by using a *framework*—a simple and flexible set of guidelines to help you structure your approach. The complexity of the method should match the importance and complexity of your problem.

- *Questioning approach.* Use basic questions to help investigate the problem and find an appropriate solution.
- *Simple framework.* Use three simple steps to help you solve your problem:
  1. What are you trying to achieve?
  2. What is the *real* problem?
  3. What is the solution?
- *Project framework.* Use six, more-detailed steps:
  1. What is the problem?
  2. Why is it happening?
  3. How can I fix it?
  4. Fix it!
  5. Why did it work or not work?
  6. What next?

Extended use

Once you've mastered the tools, you can become more creative about where and how you use them.

By combining discipline and experimentation, you can find out what works best for you.

Part I

How the Post-it® Note Tools Work

It's one thing to have a set of tools. It's another thing to make them work well. So before you begin using the Post-it® Note tools for solving your difficult problems, stop and read Part I. This section will keep you from falling into some common problem-solving traps and will help make the tools work well for you.

Using Post-it® Notes?

1 Understanding Problems

Problems come in all shapes and sizes. Many problems have common characteristics that can be addressed with the Post-it® Note tools described in Part II of this book. You may be launching a new advertising campaign, investigating production line rejects or planning a dinner party. Each situation contains pieces of information that can be found and organized. Doing this makes solving the problem both easier and more enjoyable.

This chapter describes these pieces of information, and how to find them and fit them together into patterns so you can make effective decisions to solve those difficult problems.

Sales are falling

I wish it were summer

Customers are complaining

My salary has not gone up this year

The car keeps breaking down

Jim looks sick

Oil prices are rising

Jane is pregnant

Memory chips are scarce

Sarah likes Mike

The weather is fine

Red and black look nice together

Business is booming

RamCo looks like a good buy

Pieces of information
(Is this everything? What do they all _mean?_)

Chunks

The connection between problems and the way we understand them can be described in one word—chunks.

What is a chunk?

The human mind is continuously being battered with vast amounts of information—so how do we cope with it? The answer is that we divide it into digestible chunks. Thus, when you look out of the window, instead of seeing a mass of shapes and colors, you recognize a tree, a road or a car. Each of these is a "chunk" that your mind can interpret as a single item.

Problems and information can also be viewed in distinct chunks. You can describe each chunk in a brief statement or phrase, such as "capture imagination of young people," "casing often fractures" or "provide smooth flow of entertainment."

You can deal with a problem by recognizing and organizing its component chunks in ways that will reveal new and interesting information chunks. These new chunks help you make decisions and identify the important actions that will solve the problem.

Using the Post-it® Note tools described in this book we write one chunk on each Note. The Notes' unique ability to be detached and re-attached enables us to move them around to form meaningful structures and relationships.

This book is written in chunks too. Each topic forms a single visual chunk to help you understand it in one reading.

What makes a good chunk?

Each Note contains a single chunk of information that is easy to read and understand.

Chunks of information on Notes often have a basic verb-noun or adjective-noun structure. They say what is happening to what:

> For example, "Broken fixture" or "Unhappy customer."

You may add information that helps describe the situation, but the whole chunk must still be clear and concise:

> For example, "Broken fixture on bath" or "Customer unhappy about delays."

A good example:
> "Many customer complaints about service delays."

Not-so-good examples:
> "Many complaints"

> "There have been quite a few telephone calls from people who have complained loudly, going on and on about how long it takes to get someone's attention so their problem can be fixed."

Finding and choosing chunks

Two common situations may arise when you are problem-solving. Either you may have too little information or you may have plenty of information, but can make little sense of it. In the first situation, the initial task must be to find the information chunks that will help you solve the problem. In the latter situation, you may want to find the important pieces that will require further attention.

Finding chunks

When you are looking for information chunks, be they problems, causes or solutions, there is a common tendency to identify only the obvious. Many people, for example, will jump rapidly to what they believe is the one good solution. This is wrong. There are usually many good solutions and the key to finding the best solution is first to find a number of good alternatives.

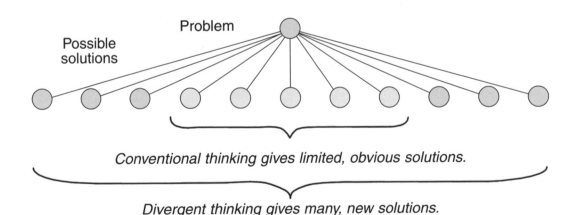

Conventional thinking gives limited, obvious solutions.

Divergent thinking gives many, new solutions.

Divergence in problem-solving

This *divergent* approach will help you find more information chunks than "conventional" thinking will. To be a successful divergent thinker, you must break down the habitual thinking patterns most people use to make their lives easier to understand and control.

Post-it® Note tools can help with divergence. The Post-up—brainstorming random chunks—is particularly good for *creative* divergence, when you are looking for new and original ideas. The Top-down Tree is good for *logical* divergence, when you are breaking down a problem into its parts. Maps can help stimulate *relational* divergence (which may be logical or creative).

Who make good divergent thinkers?

- Children, who haven't been conditioned into conventional thinking.
- Comedians, who find unexpected fun in ordinary situations.
- International negotiators, who find agreeable solutions to extreme differences.

You, when you set your mind free.

Choosing chunks

The *divergent approach* will help you identify many chunks. But then you must make sense of it all and choose which specific chunks to act on. This transition, from having many chunks to a few (often just one), is called *convergence.*

A divergent activity is almost always followed by a convergent activity. You sort the wheat from the chaff, selecting those items to act on further. A long problem-solving process can be kept manageable this way. By using divergence and convergence techniques at each stage, you'll find and keep working on the best alternative.

One danger of convergence is that people may become too conservative. They choose only obvious, logical and safe solutions. The answer is to remain logical, but avoid throwing the baby out with the bath water. Ask careful questions and don't rush to a decision.

Post-it® Note tools can help with convergence. Trees and maps are useful for organizing and understanding the information you have collected. The *Bottom-up Tree*—which groups many chunks into a few categories—is perfect for convergence from a large list of chunks. The *Swap Sort*—prioritizing chunks by comparing them in pairs—is good for choosing from among a shorter list of items. These tools are discussed in more detail in Part II.

Who make good convergent thinkers?

- Judges, who weigh the pros and cons of an argument.
- Researchers, who patiently sort through piles of data.

You, when you focus on what's important.

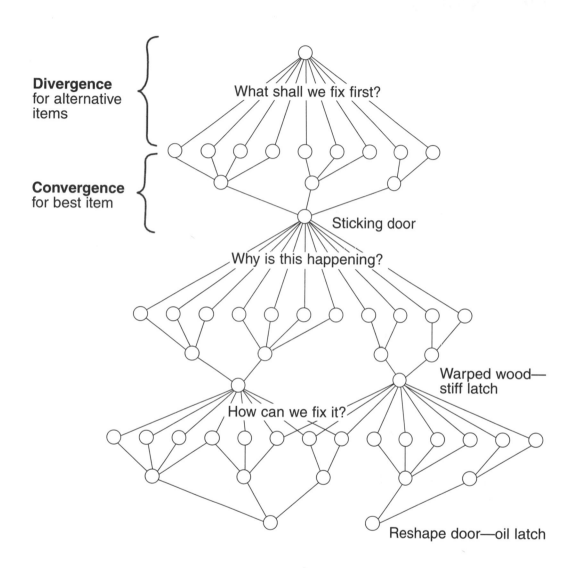

Divergence
for alternative
items

Convergence
for best item

What shall we fix first?

Sticking door

Why is this happening?

Warped wood—
stiff latch

How can we fix it?

Reshape door—oil latch

**Example of divergence and convergence
sequence in problem-solving**

How chunks fit together

In order to make sense of the many chunks that are created with divergent activities such as the Post-up, we begin by looking at how they may be related. At a basic level, there are three structures we can create: the list, the tree and the map.

Lists

The simplest way to group information chunks is to list them, one after the other. The Post-up results in a list of chunks, arranged in no particular order. They are related only by the fact that a common set of rules was used to find them all.

The next step beyond the nonordered list is the ordered list. Take the results of a Post-up or any other tool and ask the question, "Which is most important?" Then create a list with the most important Note at the top, followed by the next most important and so on, with the least important Note at the bottom. The Swap Sort can be used to produce this prioritized list.

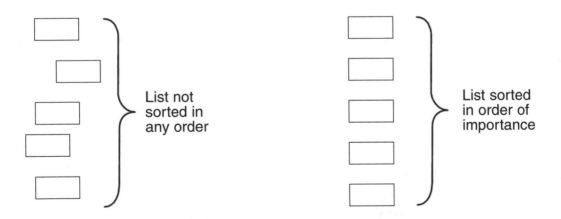

Lists show nonordered or ordered simple groups

Trees

Chunks are usually made up of other, smaller chunks. A car includes a door, which includes a handle, which includes a lever, and so on.

Chunking works in both directions. Given a piece of information, you can both "chunk down" by breaking it into its constituent parts, or "chunk up" by finding what it is a part of. Thus, "cracked pipe" can be chunked down to "stressed in operation" and "weak joint," or chunked up to "machine failure."

Connecting these different levels of chunks forms a tree-shaped structure. The two directions of chunking give us the two varieties of tree tool: the Top-down Tree and the Bottom-up Tree.

Trees appear in many situations. Sometimes the situation naturally contains a tree, such as an organizational chart. Often, chunking on different levels fits the way our minds work. When writing a book, for example, the main structure may be determined first, followed by chapters, sections and subsections.

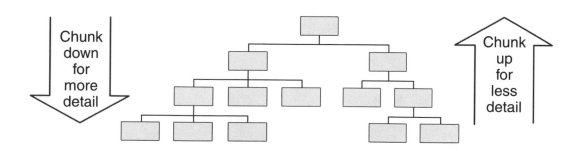

Trees show hierarchical relationships

Maps

In some situations, the information chunks have more complex relationships than trees can show. The human mind is quite good at dealing with this type of situation. People fit random chunks into familiar patterns, often using a known set of rules. For example, when talking with a group of people, we will combine what we know about the topic of conversation with what we know about each person. Thus, we alter what we say and how we say it.

Similarly, we can build chunks of information into complex maps to help us understand a situation better. These maps differ from each other, and from hierarchies, in the *type* of relationship they express between individual chunks. For example, when the chunks are people, the relationship may be one of friendship, a business structure and so on.

The relationship between tasks or actions is common in maps, as shown in the Action Map (see chapter 9). The Information Map (see chapter 8) is used to show any other general relationships. A common example is how chunks are caused by other chunks.

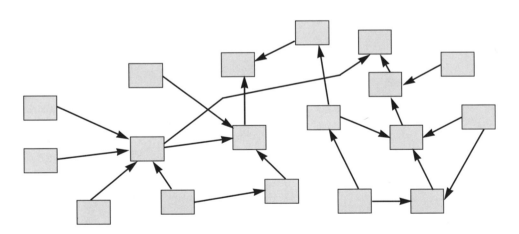

Maps show complex interrelationships

2 Making Decisions

When finding and organizing information chunks, you are continually making decisions. But how do you recognize those decision points? And how do you know if you are making the right decision?

There are two important factors to consider that will help you make decisions more effectively:

- First, how do you decide what information to collect? How do you know how to put it together? How do you decide which parts are important? Without guidance, you can easily make decisions that point you in the wrong direction.
- Second, how true is the information on which you are basing your decisions? If you are using inaccurate information, then your decisions are unlikely to give the right answer. As the saying goes: "Garbage in, garbage out."

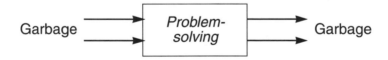

Garbage in = Garbage out

Guiding lights

In order to help you find the right information chunks in a session, to help organize them and to make the right decisions afterwards, you need some kind of direction, some guiding light.

A simple set of guidelines will help you identify and put together the right information chunks, and then decide on the right subsequent actions.

Objectives

It has been said that if you aim at nothing, you will probably hit it. You can often see this in problem-solving situations, where people are working hard, but don't seem to achieve anything.

The minimum guideline for any activity is writing a "statement of objectives" describing what you are trying to achieve. This provides the main guiding light for all other actions and decisions. The statement must be clear and concise. It should also be easy to tell when the objective has been met.

Written objectives are particularly useful when working with other people. The statement provides a "contract of agreement" and ensures that everyone is working in the same direction.

A clear objective:

Reduce clerical errors on outbound invoices by 50% by the end of May.

An unclear objective:

Reduce errors.

Criteria

If you ask ten people to choose a good piece of music, they will each choose differently because they each judge music by different standards.

You can make better, more acceptable decisions by clarifying your criteria for each decision.

The basic criterion for any decision is that it helps to achieve the objectives. Other criteria form sub-objectives that help the lower-level decisions. For example, if the objective is to "select a plant to put in the garden," criteria may include "stays green all year" and "resistant to aphids."

Questions

One of the best ways to direct activities when problem-solving is to ask good questions. These questions should give strong direction or prompt further thinking in different directions.

Questioning can form the basis of a complete approach to problem-solving (see chapter 10).

Other guidelines

Other guidelines that can help your decision-making include *nonobjectives* that clarify the boundaries of the basic objectives. *Constraints* limit what you can do.

When writing objectives, criteria and other guidelines, always try to keep a balance between brevity and detail. The bottom line is they should *help*, not hinder, your decision-making.

The FOG factor

A simple and effective way of identifying the quality of information chunks is to classify them into Facts, Opinions or Guesses. If you take the first letter of each of these words, they spell "FOG," which provides a useful way of remembering them. (If it's not clear how true a chunk is, your confidence in it is likely to be pretty "foggy.")

Facts

Facts are undeniable and are capable of being proved. They are the best form of information, but are surprisingly rare.

The usual way of finding facts is by measuring. This can involve qualitative questioning or quantitative physical measurement. What you measure will depend on the question you want to answer.

Facts are seldom free. To prove that customers like a new product feature, for example, you will have to spend time to go out and ask them.

Facts are not always expensive. Sometimes a simple cross-check will tell you exactly what you want to know. For example, if you think that a board is 7 feet long, you can easily prove it with a measuring tape.

The key to using facts is to balance the potential benefit of knowing with the cost of finding out. It is easy to go too far in either direction, either by wasting time on those last few percentage points or by claiming that it is "just not worth the effort."

When problem-solving, it is important to identify opinions and guesses that, if proven to be facts, are valuable enough to warrant further action.

Opinions

Opinions are the most common form of information. They are the considered thoughts of people. They may also be facts that just can't be proven.

Opinions have the widest range of possible truth. They can be based on long and practical experience, uncertain rumors, or even outright prejudice.

One problem with opinions is that people who have them tend to think of them as facts, even when they're not. If their opinions are respected, then other people may also treat them as facts. Opinions should be recognized as opinions and treated with caution.

An important part of problem-solving lies not only in differentiating between facts and opinions, but also in exploring opinions and finding out how people have come to their conclusions.

Guesses

Guesses, on the other hand, are acknowledged as uncertain ideas. During divergent activities, like brainstorming, guesses help expand the area of interest.

They often appear in Post-up sessions when you're looking for creative new concepts.

Most guesses turn out to be untrue and of little value, so why use them? Because those few that *are* valuable tend to provide a significant breakthrough. Guesses can be the most useless *and* the most useful part of solving problems.

Using the FOG factor

When problem-solving, consider each chunk by asking, "What is the FOG factor?" and mark it accordingly. You can either use different Note colors (blue = Fact, yellow = Opinion, red = Guess) or write the letters F, O or G in one corner of the Note.

Then you can research and perform experiments to find which guesses and opinions are facts. For example, a guess that customers might like bright-green shoes may be followed by a survey of customer opinion. Also, a market test can determine whether such shoes would actually sell.

Note that not all problem situations require the application of the FOG factor. When the information chunks are the same type, there is no need to mark all Notes with the same letter. For example, in a creative Post-up, all chunks might be guesses. In a Top-down Tree, all chunks might be opinions.

FOG factors

- Facts are proven.
- Opinions are believed to be true by individuals.
- Guesses are recognized as uncertain ideas.

Work to convert opinions and guesses into facts.

Part II
The Post-it® Note Tool Box

The Post-it® Note tool box consists of three classes of tools. Each class contains two separate tools, as shown in the tree below. The chapters in this part provide easy steps for using each tool. Part III then gives some examples of how the tools may be used together to solve actual problems.

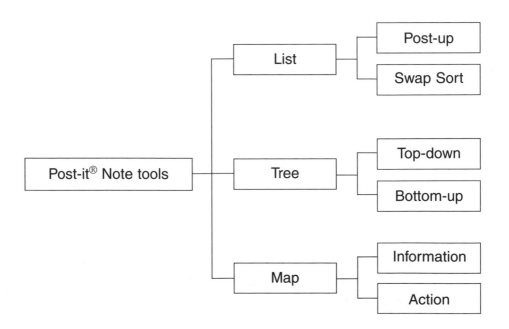

The Post-it® Note Tool Box

Post-it® Note tools

3 Using the Post-it® Note Tools

Whenever you use Post-it® Note tools to solve problems, you should use a common set of actions, or steps. Although they aren't directly related to any one tool, each step will contribute to the successful use of all tools.

In summary, these steps are:

1. Identify the objective of using the tool.
2. Identify other guidelines to help meet the objective.
3. Determine where the information can be found.
4. Assemble a team to work on the problem.
5. Prepare for the meeting.
6. Use the tool to gather and organize the information.
7. Use the results to achieve the objective.

1. Identify objective

Identify the objective of using the tool by describing, as simply as possible, what you are trying to achieve. For example:

- Find the main causes of customer dissatisfaction.
- Decide what present to give John for his birthday.
- Reduce invoicing costs by 10%.
- Assign tasks for rebuilding furnaces.

Identifying your objective will help you to decide on other actions while using the tool. It also helps you know when to stop. No more work is needed when the objective has been met.

2. Identify constraints, nonobjectives and questions

Identify any additional information that may help keep you on the right track. This may include the following:

- *Constraints*, which limit what you can do. They usually involve cost, time or resources.
- *Nonobjectives.* What you are *not* trying to achieve. They might be mistaken for objectives.
- *Questions* to ask yourself when creating and moving Notes. You only get the right answer if you ask the right question.

Examples:
Constraint: Task must be done by end of January and be within current budget.
Nonobjective: Reducing space usage (when no extra space is needed).
Question: What is a direct cause of this?

3. Find where the information is

Determine where to find the information you need to meet your objective. If it is in reports, minutes, books, and so on, then take a pad of Post-it® Notes and do some research.

If the required information is not written down or easily available, identify a team of people who can work together to dig it up.

4. Select the team

When choosing team members, make sure they can all contribute in some way. Together, they should have (or have access to) all the necessary information.

Try to choose people who will work well together. Their knowledge and thinking style should match the problem. Some problems require more creative thinking, while others need a more logical approach.

A smaller team is usually more effective than a larger team. Three or four people is good, although up to around ten can work satisfactorily.

Make sure everyone is comfortable using the Post-it® Note tools. You could provide a separate training session or a short presentation during the meeting. Either way, be available to help as they learn to use the tools.

Use a facilitator or a group member who is reasonably expert in using the tools and is able to show the others what to do. If everyone is new to the tools, be prepared to go more slowly. You probably won't achieve perfect results the first time.

5. Set up the working area

Before the meeting, set up three vertically mounted areas, as shown in the diagram on page 25, that everyone can see and access.

The Help page is typically a flipchart, placed to one side. This contains the objective from Step 1. Also include other hints or constraints that will help the team to focus and identify useful chunks and relationships.

The Work Area is where most of the Notes will be stuck, so it needs to be large and central. A dry-erase board works well because you can draw and redraw lines between Notes. An alternative, which can be taken away from the meeting room, is several sheets of flipchart paper, taped together.

The Store is simply an area next to the Work Area for putting Notes that aren't a part of the current diagram. It may contain Notes from an initial Post-up or ones that have been temporarily removed from the Work Area.

When the Work Area starts overflowing, the Store also provides a useful "secondary" Work Area in which to continue the diagram. Use letter codes (such as a capital "A" in a circle) to show the link point in the Work Area and the continuation point in the Store.

Because most sessions are active, you'll need to have sufficient space in front of these areas for everyone to move around freely. There should be pads of Post-it® Notes and markers or pens on tables nearby. Arrange chairs in a semicircle farther back.

Help

Objectives, constraints and other prompts to help achieve an effective session.

Store

Temporary storage of Notes and a secondary work area.

Work Area

Main working area where Notes are organized in the session.

Setting up for Post-it® Note session

6. Use the tool to organize information

Use the tool, as described in the following chapters, to create or organize your information.

7. Use results to meet the objective

After using the tool, spend some time making sure you have the right information. Then use it to achieve your objective.

In creative activities, if you have the time, leave the Notes in place for several days to let ideas "incubate." Then, go back from time to time just to look, adding or changing Notes as desired.

For more-logical activities or when you have made assumptions, verify the facts and assumptions by performing various experiments, asking people, taking measurements and so on.

When you're comfortable with the final diagram, put it onto paper and give everyone a copy. It will serve as a concise documentation of the decision-making process you have used. You can refer to it later when you succeed (or don't) in meeting your objective.

4 The Post-up

What is it for?

To collect pieces of information about a situation.

When Do I Use It?

To gather individual chunks of information about a problem situation. This tool is especially useful when that information is not written down neatly in one place (this happens in most problems!).

It's commonly used when the information is held in people's heads. Each individual in the group knows something about part of the problem, but not all of it.

The Post-up can also be used to collect various written information from reports, documents, journals and so on.

Use this tool, instead of conventional brainstorming, for easier and quicker generation of creative new ideas.

By itself, the Post-up does nothing with the information that it creates. You should use it with other Post-it® Note tools to help make useful decisions. You can use the Post-up *while* you use another tool, building a problem diagram as you go. Or you can set up two separate sessions: First do a Post-up, then use a second tool to organize the results.

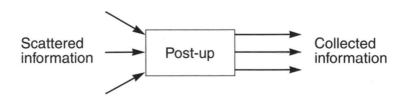

How does it work?

Information about a problem is often scattered and unclear. It may be in various places, such as old reports and meeting minutes. It may not be written down but found only by asking the right questions of a number of people.

Collecting this information together in one place enables you to review and understand it as a whole, especially if each piece is a uniform and discrete chunk. Once collected, these chunks may then be organized relative to one another to reveal further useful information.

The Post-up involves writing down each piece of information on a Note, then sticking it up with others. The result is a large sheet of paper, a dry-erase board or a wall covered in Notes.

The Post-up works best when used with a team of people because it actively involves everyone in writing and posting. Compared with traditional brainstorming meetings, where one person stands at the front writing down thoughts as they are called out, the Post-up has several beneficial effects:

- *Efficient use of time.* No one has to wait for a turn before giving suggestions.
- *Effective data collection.* Everyone is involved, all of the time. No one can sit back and let the others do the work.
- *Fair play.* No one person dominates. Independent action means everyone is equal.
- *Relative anonymity.* Focus on individuals is reduced; focus on the problem is increased.

Minimizing talk during the Post-up session contributes to all of the above, enabling each person to concentrate on the task at hand. It also helps in creative sessions, where it encourages the use of the nonverbal, creative parts of the brain.

Also, because you may not collect all the information you need in one session, the Post-up tool allows for an "incubation" period during which new Post-it® Notes may be added.

The Post-up

How do I do it?

1. Identify objective

Identify your objective and set up the meeting as described in chapter 3. Here are some typical Post-up objectives:

- How can the cassette case be made 10% thinner?
- What is the factual (not circumstantial) evidence in the case of the State vs. Jones?
- What boys' names do we like?
- What do we know about the Acme release plans?

In a creative session, the following considerations may help:

- Hold the meeting somewhere informal, outside the normal working environment.
- Don't invite people who will inhibit the others (for example, the boss).
- Stimulate the creative juices beforehand with a game.
- Add "thought trigger" questions to the Help area to prompt creative thinking. They can be single words, or longer sentences or phrases. For example:
  —Replace?
  —Extend?
  —Rearrange?
  —Reduce or simplify?
  —Combine items?
  —Change the sequence?

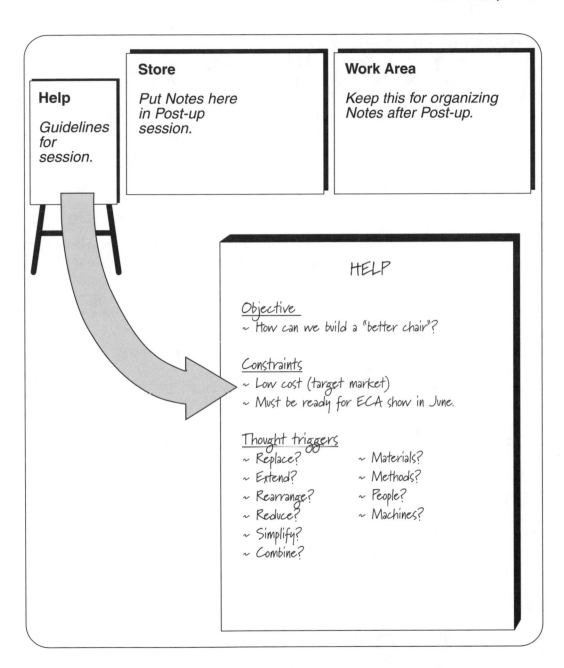

Setting up for the post-up session

2. Stick Post-it® Notes in the store

Give each person a Post-it® Note pad and a felt-tip pen and then proceed with the Post-up as follows:

- Each participant writes statements or phrases that help to answer the question from Step 1. They put one statement on one note. Then they stick it up in the Store. (The Work Area is kept clear for organizing the notes afterwards, using another tool.)
- If the Notes contain a mixture of facts, opinions and guesses, then these differences should be indicated. Use different Note colors (blue = Fact, yellow = Opinion, red = Guess) or write the letter F, O or G in the top righthand corner of each Note. A fact can be proved, an opinion is believed to be true, a guess is simply an idea.
- No talking is allowed during the Post-up. The only exception may be an occasional question to clarify the meaning of something written on a Note.
- Keep challenging yourselves for new things to post:
  —Look at other Notes.
  —Look at the objectives and questions on the Help area.
  —Take a break, then come back refreshed.

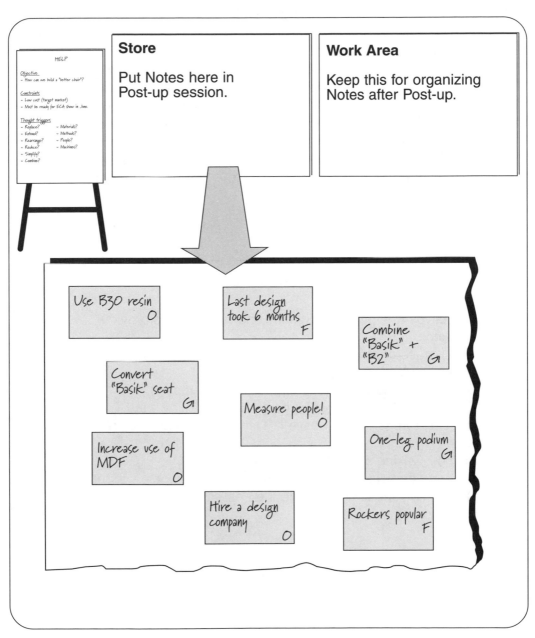

Posting up information chunks

3. Use the results as planned

When everyone has run out of ideas to post up, either close the session or move on to using the Post-up Notes with another tool.

If you have the time and space, leave the Post-up in place for a few days. Return to it over the next week or so, adding new Notes as more information is found or ideas appear. If appropriate, you can even leave it in a public place, encouraging visitors to add their own thoughts.

This incubation period also lets the validity of these thoughts and ideas sink in before you make further judgments about them.

Post-up Keys

- Objectives and questions clearly shown nearby to provide guidance.
- One phrase or statement per Note. Make it easy for everyone to understand.
- Discriminate between facts, opinions and guesses.
- Everyone works together. Write a Note and stick it up!
- Once a Note is posted, leave it. They can be moved or removed later.
- Silence. Talking steals focus from the Post-up.
- Look at other Notes and think. Play off other people's thoughts.
- When everyone is done, leave the Post-up for a while. Keep coming back to add more.

5 The Swap Sort

What is it for?

To help you prioritize a list of items.

When Do I Use It?

When you have a disorganized list of items that you want to sort in order of importance. For example, use the Swap Sort when you have a list of possible actions and you want to choose only one or two to pursue.

A short list of items (around ten or fewer) is best. The Swap Sort can be time-consuming when it is used to sort a long list. Long lists can be used if they're reduced as described in this chapter.

The Swap Sort is useful when a group of people cannot agree on which items are most important. It forces them to tackle the problem in a more organized way.

It is typically used after other Post-it® Note tools, either directly after a Post-up or when a shorter list has been selected from a Tree or Map.

How does it work?

Often, when working on a problem, you have a number of information chunks you want to rank in order of importance. Or you need to choose one or two to act on. For example, you may find many ways to reduce insect infestation, but then how do you choose the best one to use?

This problem is addressed with the Swap Sort, which puts a disorganized list of items into order of importance.

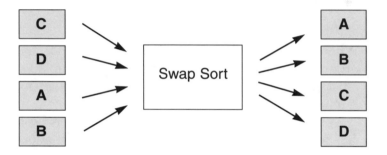

Before starting to prioritize, you must ask, "What makes one item more important than another?" Different people may use different criteria and will disagree about the importance of each item. To avoid this, first you must agree on a list of selection criteria as a consistent way of judging each item.

The Swap Sort works by comparing pairs of Notes in a list, then swapping them if they are in the wrong positions. This is done over and over until all the Notes in the list are ranked in proper order. Comparing Notes in pairs against defined criteria makes the decision of "which is more important" much easier. It's also more likely to give better results than simply plucking the Notes out of a large group.

If the list is almost in order, few swaps will be needed. On the other hand, a list in reverse order can require more swaps before it is sorted out. The maximum number of swaps increases sharply with the number of items in the list, as shown in the table below. Therefore, it is quicker to shorten a long list before starting to swap.

Number of items in list	Maximum number of swaps
2	1
3	3
5	10
10	45
20	190

Swap Sort

How do I do it?

1. Identify objective

Identify your objective and set up the meeting as described in chapter 3. For example:

- Select which probable causes of engine failure to investigate.
- Decide which articles to write and in which order.
- Find the winner of the violin competition.
- Identify features to include in the new product.

2. Create prioritization criteria

Use the objective from Step 1 to create the prioritization criteria to use when comparing the Notes. Typical criteria are:

- Costs little to implement
- Easy to do (we have the skills)
- Follows the defined standards or rules
- Quick to do
- No need to involve other people (do it ourselves)
- Easy to persuade other people

Phrase the criteria to make agreeing with them desirable—"quick to do" rather than "speed of implementation."

There should be very few criteria. One is ideal, three are acceptable, more will make later decisions increasingly difficult.

When the criteria and *their* order of importance are not clear, you can use a mini Post-up and Swap Sort to find and sort them into order (using the objective to compare them).

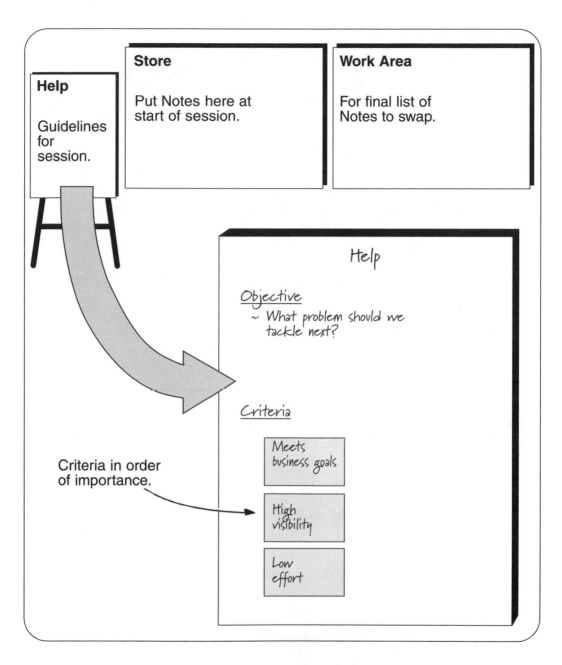

Setting up criteria for swap sort

3. Gather Notes

Gather the items you want to sort, each written on one Note, and put them in the Store area. They may come from a Post-up or be a selection of key items from a Tree or Map.

4. Reduce size of long lists

If there are more than ten Notes to sort, reduce them as follows:

- Compare each Note against the objective and criteria. Decide whether it is worth keeping or may be rejected now as a low-priority item. If it's worth keeping, transfer it to the Work Area.
- Look for pairs of Notes that repeat each other or can be combined. Either put one Note to one side or stick both Notes together.

Another way of quickly reducing even a very large list is to ask everyone to select a fixed number of Notes (five, for example) to carry forward to a new, smaller list. If necessary, repeat several times to shorten the list further.

5. Arrange Notes in a vertical list

Arrange the Notes in the Work Area into a vertical list. (They will be sorted into order of importance in the next step, so don't try to sort them now!)

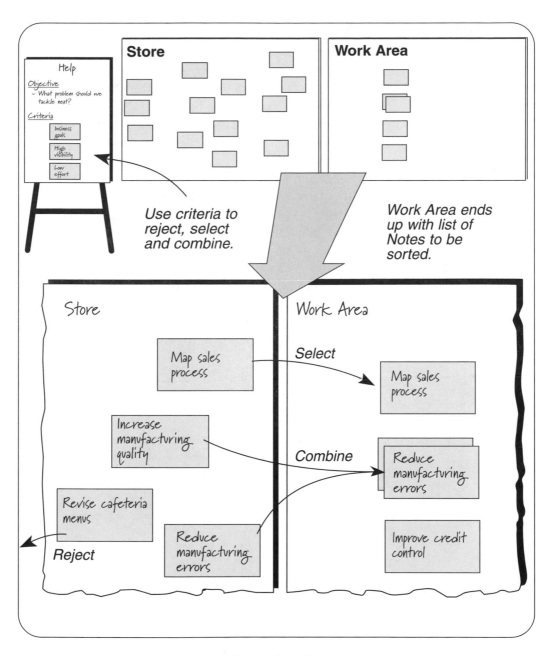

List reduction

6. Swap pairs of Notes

Compare and swap pairs of Notes using the following process:

- Compare the first two Notes at the top of the list, using the criteria from Step 2. If the lower one is more important than the higher one, then swap their positions in the list.
- Compare the next two Notes in the list (including the second in the list, which you just compared, plus the next Note down, number three in the list). As in the previous comparison, if they are in the wrong order, swap them.
- Repeat this comparing and swapping of Notes until you reach the bottom of the list. If there are five Notes in the list, you will compare one and two, then two and three, then three and four, then four and five.
- If any pair of Notes was swapped in this pass through the list, repeat the process and keep repeating it until you can go through the complete list without swapping any pairs.

Thus, the sequence for sorting a list of letters could look like this:

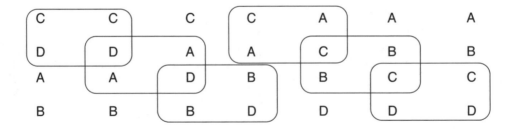

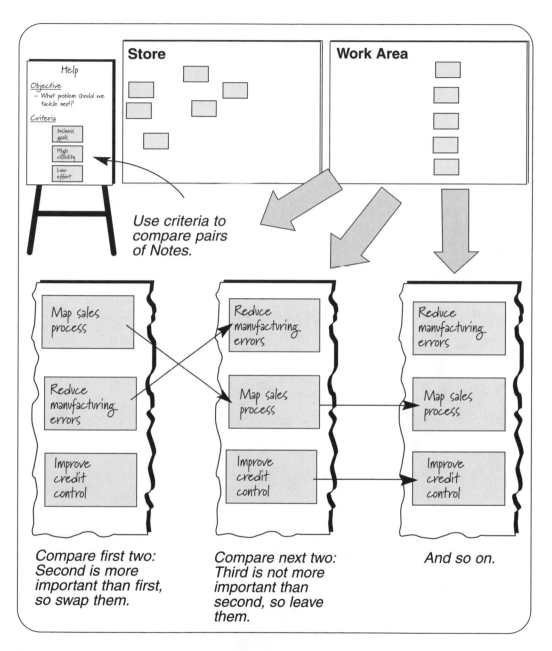

Sorting into order

7. Use list as planned

The Notes are now in order of importance according to your criteria. Use the list as planned in your original objective.

Swap-Sort Keys

- Agree on what "important" means.
- Reduce the list to ten Notes or less.
- Put the Notes vertically above one another.
- Compare pairs of Notes (starting from the top and working down).
- If the lower Note of a pair is more important than the higher one, then swap their positions in the list.
- Repeat the process until you can't find any more pairs to swap.

---

6 The Top-down Tree

What is it for?

To break down a problem into a useful set of parts.

When Do I Use It?

When investigating a problem (or an interesting part of it) that you can describe with a simple statement.

When designing something, from a house to an essay, it is useful to identify its individual components. Similarly, with an existing item, such as a competitor's product, you can use this same process to figure out how it is made.

Another common use for the Top-down Tree is to find out why something is happening. In this case, use the tree to identify possible causes for a known effect. You can also reverse this process when looking for possible solutions to a problem, finding out how a desired effect may be caused.

When you plan a project, you can use the Top-down Tree to break down large tasks into units that are easily allocated and managed.

Use it instead of a Bottom-up Tree when the general problem is understood and more information is needed about the details rather than the big picture.

Use it instead of an Information Map to do a logical breakdown of the problem, rather than a more creative investigation of relationships.

How does it work?

In many situations, you have a just a little information, possibly only a simple description of the problem. You then need to find out more detail about the problem. You need to expand upon it or dig deeper to find useful information.

The Top-down Tree breaks down a single problem chunk into layers of more detailed chunks by repeatedly asking a simple, well-defined question. It enables you to build up a consistent and complete picture of the problem. Also, because only one chunk is dealt with at one time, it can make a complex problem much easier to handle.

When you are working on a problem with clear boundaries, use a structured set of questions to break down the tree. This helps make sure that the complete problem, no more and no less, is mapped.

The Top-down Tree can help improve your understanding of a problem. As you are breaking down the tree, you "unfold" the problem one level at a time. This allows you to explore and understand it better than if you had gone right into its most minute details. This way, you can carefully examine each layer, one at a time, before you go on to the next. It's as though you are peeling away an onion, one layer at a time, to find the center—in this case, the source of your problem.

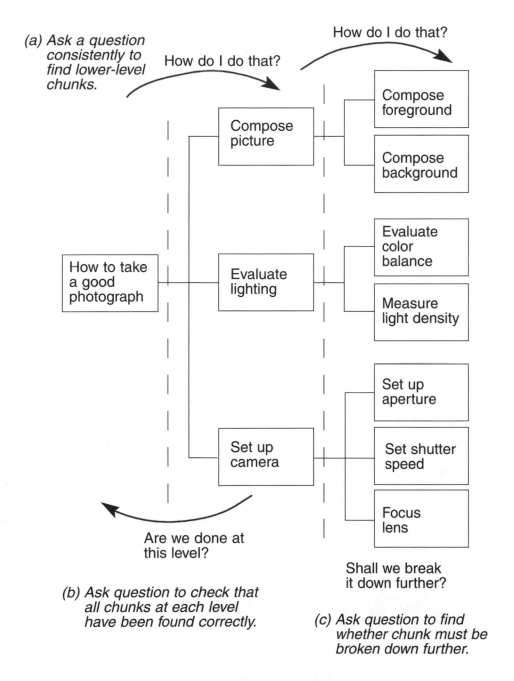

Top-down Tree

A number of common words are used to describe different parts of a tree. Most of them come from parts of a family tree or from parts of the more familiar, wooden variety.

- A single item is sometimes called a *node* (the lumpy part of a plant or tree where the leaf joins the main stem).
- The one top-level node is called the *root,* because all other items stem from it.
- A *parent* has one or more *children* items beneath it.
- A *child* has one parent only. All nodes except the root are children. This parent–child structure is known as a *hierarchy.* This characteristic distinguishes trees from maps.
- A *leaf* is a bottom-level node that has no children of its own.
- All children of one parent are often (but not always) considered together as a *family* because in combination they are equivalent to the parent. In such cases, all leaves together represent the root.

For example, if the tree is used to break down a vehicle into its parts, the leaves will contain all the individual components that are required to build the vehicle.

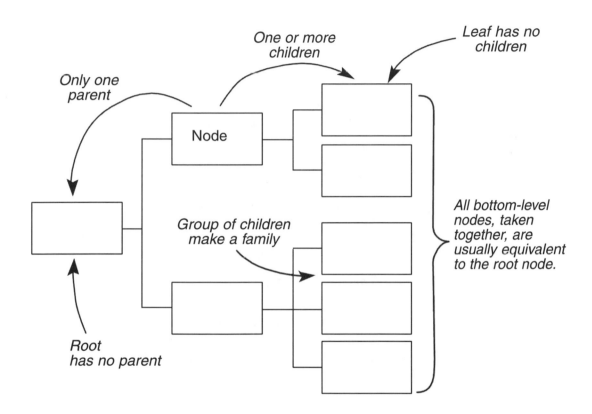

Parts of a Tree

Whichever way the tree is built, the result is always a hierarchy. You can represent a hierarchy in a number of ways. The approach you take depends on the type of problem you are solving, the space available for sticking up Notes and maybe individual preference.

This book consistently uses a left-to-right layout, but there is no reason why you should not use any of the other possible approaches. Do your own experiments. Use the table below to help you decide which methods best fit your problem-solving situations.

Tree Shape	When Tree May Be Useful
Top-down	Good for simple trees, but you may run out of horizontal space, especially in a narrow Work Area. Combine with a comb shape when there are many leaves.
Star	Useful when there are many children at each level, but can become messy when families start to merge.
Left-to-Right	Easy to distinguish levels, but you may run out of vertical space when there are many children in families.
Inside-out	Useful layout for the Bottom-up Tree. Not recommended for Top-down Tree.
Comb	Useful with a long, narrow Work Area (such as several separate flipchart sheets).
Fishbone	A flexible variant of left-to-right, but families in middle of diagram may run out of space.

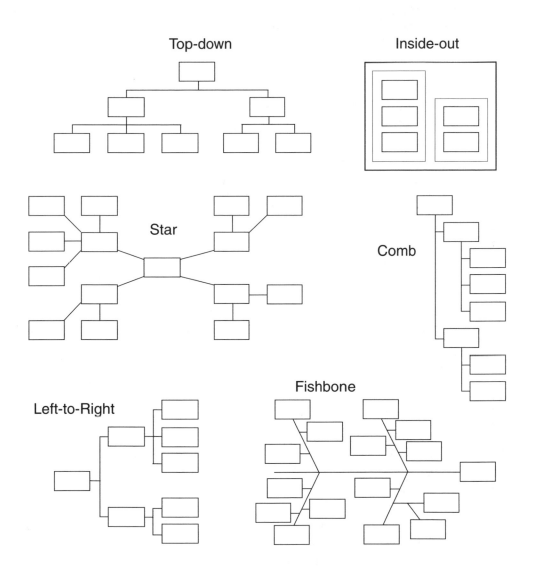

Top-down

Inside-out

Star

Comb

Left-to-Right

Fishbone

Tree Layouts

How do I do it?

1. Identify objectives

Identify objectives and the people involved, and set up the meeting as described in chapter 3. Some typical objectives:

- Find key reasons why wood in storage shed B is warping.
- Define the roles needed in the new organization.
- Identify tasks for assembly of Maximan radio.

2. Identify "Help" questions

Use the objectives to identify questions to ask while building the tree, then write these in the Help Area. There are three questions you can use:

(a) To ask of a parent that will help you identify its children. For example, "What would directly cause this?"

(b) To ask of children to make sure they've all been correctly identified. For example, "Do all children, taken together, completely represent the parent?"

(c) To ask of a Note, to determine whether you need to find its children. When the answer is "No" for all childless Notes, you have completed the tree. For example, "Can this task be completed within one week?" or "Do I need to know more detail?"

It can sometimes be useful to change question (a) at a defined point in the tree. When no causes can be found, for example, change "What causes this?" to "How can it be fixed?"

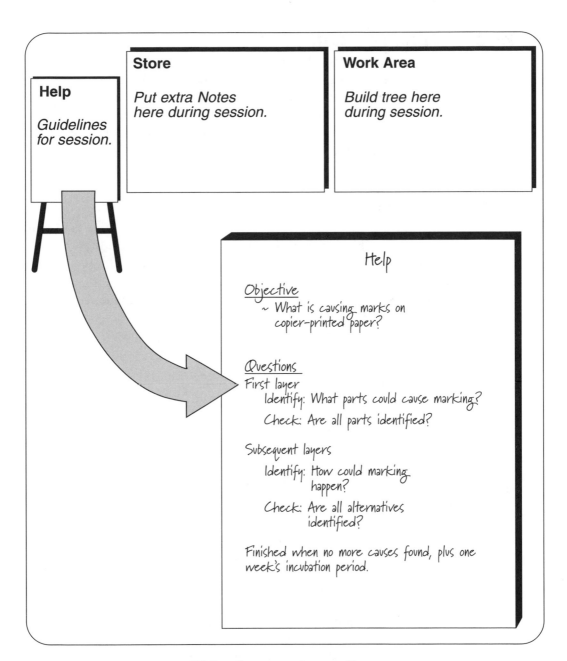

Objectives and questions

3. Write root problem statement

Use the objective from Step 1 to write a clear and unambiguous problem statement or question on a Note. This forms the root Note of the tree. For example, an objective like "Identify causes of office overheating" may result in a root problem of "office is overheating."

Stick this up in the Work Area in a position where the rest of the tree can flow from it. Where you put it will depend on how you intend to shape the tree (see page 51).

4. Identify children

Identify the children of the root Note by asking question (a) from Step 2. Write each child item on one Note and stick it up in the Work Area. Put the Note near the root problem, but spaced widely enough for following children to be positioned.

Ask question (b) from Step 2 to find out whether you have completed the family. If not, keep asking questions.

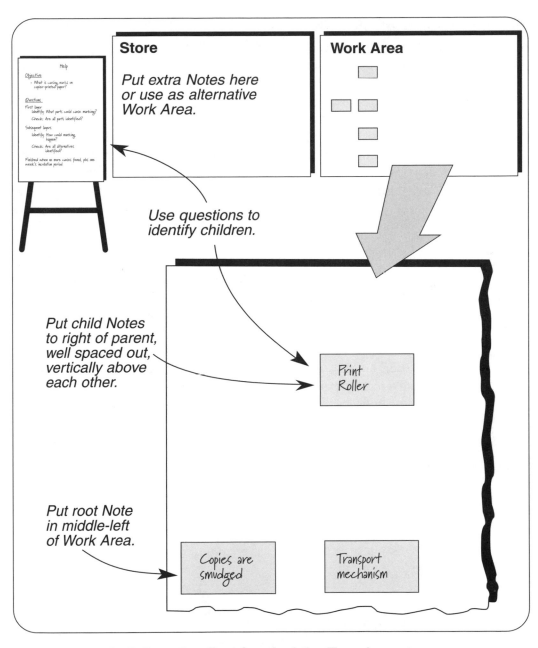

Building the first level of the Top-down tree

5. Check for completion

For each child identified in Step 4, ask question (c) from Step 2 to decide if you need to find more children. If you do, identify and position them in the Work Area as in Step 4.

Repeat this process, identifying one complete family at a time, until you cannot find any more children.

When breaking down a tree, aim for small families. They are easier to arrange and understand. Be critical of large families created at any one level. Sometimes they are a mistake. The information may be better represented by adding levels instead of leaving them squashed together as a large family. Ask of each Note, "Should this be at a lower level? Is it directly related to the parent?"

When sticking up Notes, make sure that they are positioned so that individual families can be clearly identified. Also make sure there's enough space around each Note for *its* children to be positioned.

If families collide or you run out of space to position Notes, then rearrange the tree. You can shuffle Notes and move out entire subtrees or rebuild the subtree in the Store area.

Sometimes, rearranging Notes is rather awkward. You may run out of reorganizing space or have too many Notes to move. In this case, use a felt-tip pen or marker to clarify relationships. For example, use solid lines between related Notes, reference links to connect remote subtrees and dashed lines to separate different families.

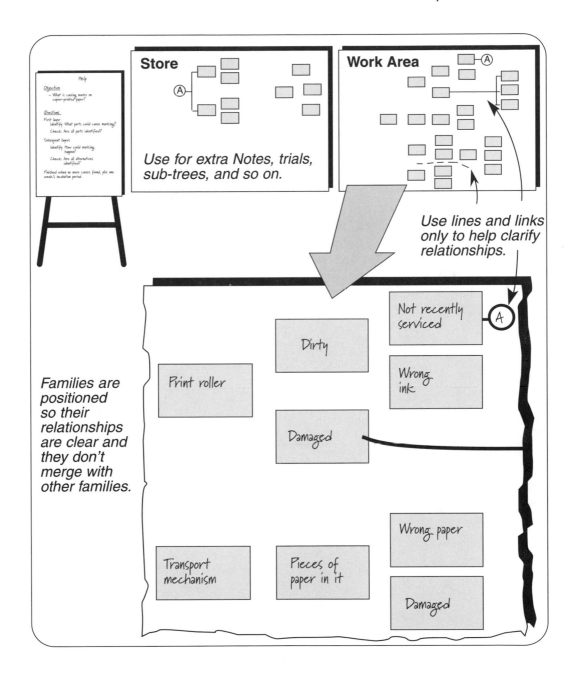

Building up the Tree

6. Add lines

While the structure of the tree is still uncertain, avoid adding lines if you can. When you are confident that the tree is correct, then add lines to highlight the family groups.

In case you do have to move Notes, use a dry-erase board for the Work Area to make it easier to erase old lines.

Adding lines makes the tree appear more complete because now you can clearly see its structure. It can also make you feel less inclined to change the tree, which is another reason to leave this step until the end.

When subtrees are continued elsewhere, such as in the Store area, show the link to them with the same circled letter at both the "jump out" and "arrive in" points. Each different link should contain a different letter.

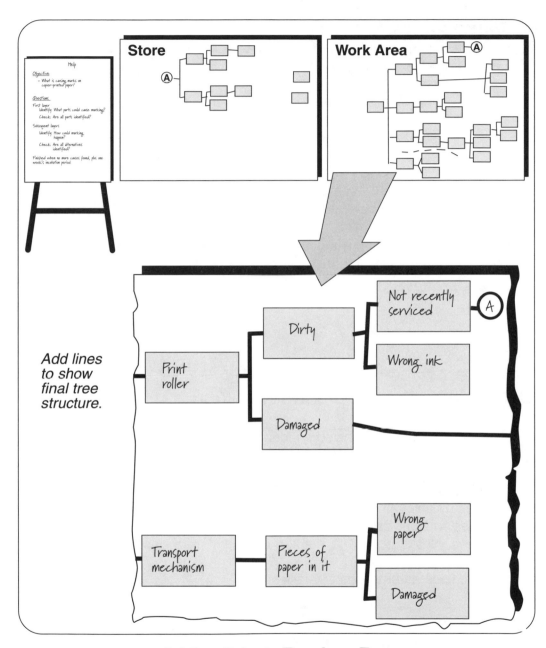

Adding links to Top-down Tree

7. Check completed tree

When the tree is finished, review it for completeness, clarity and usefulness as follows:

Completeness	Check that the questions from Step 2 are completely and correctly answered at each layer.
Clarity	Make sure that both individual Notes and relationships between parents and children are easily understood.
Usefulness	Ask whether the completed tree can be used to meet the objective from Step 1.

Put an appropriate amount of effort into this step, depending on the importance of the final results. For example, use extra effort when reviewing a breakdown of tasks for a mission-critical project.

Top-down Tree Keys

- Define questions to help you identify children, check families and decide when the tree is complete.
- Choose a tree shape. If unsure, use Left-to-Right.
- Write one item per Note, starting with the root problem.
- Identify children by consistently asking a defined question.
- Position Note families so relationships are clear.
- Move Notes or use a marker or pen if relationships become unclear.
- Add lines at end to show families.

7 The Bottom-up Tree

What is it for?

To organize many different chunks of information into a clear and coherent whole.

When do I use it?

When there are many individual pieces of information about a problem and it is not clear how they are related. The information chunks don't have to be clear and written down. They can be vague and half-thought-out. It's the job of the Bottom-up Tree to help make sense of this confusion.

The Bottom-up Tree is perfect when you are just starting to find out about a problem. The tool will help piece together the jigsaw puzzle from assorted scraps of knowledge various people have.

The Bottom-up Tree is useful for formal planning, investigations and general problem-solving. These activities often start out with vague thoughts and ideas.

Sometimes, when you've been working on a problem for a while, the tree or map you're using doesn't seem to help or reflect the true situation. In this case, you can use the Bottom-up Tree to restructure the information and give you a fresh picture of the problem.

When a group of individuals can't agree on what the real problem is, the Bottom-up Tree is useful. The group works on shared data and reaches joint conclusions about the problem.

How does it work?

It's common to have plenty of information, yet still not be any closer to solving your problem. You can't see the forest for the trees. The quantity or diversity of your information chunks seems more like a confusing maze than a clear path to a solution.

The Bottom-up Tree organizes this mess by grouping these leaves into families. These families are grouped into larger families, and so on, until all of the original pieces of information are related in a tree.

As with the Post-up, when working in a group of people, the tree is usually built in silence. This reduces diversions, such as arguments about where individual Notes should be placed. You also avoid side discussions that aren't focused on the problem at hand. When trying to look with fresh eyes at a problem, silence stimulates the creative right brain. Then you can find hidden, nonobvious ways of grouping Notes.

A Bottom-up Tree will often be pretty shallow, with a few large families and only two or three levels. There are no rules against breaking it down into more levels with smaller families.

A good Bottom-up Tree will typically weave together between 25 and 100 seemingly unrelated Notes into a new diagram. You'll find common threads that give a new shape to a poorly understood problem.

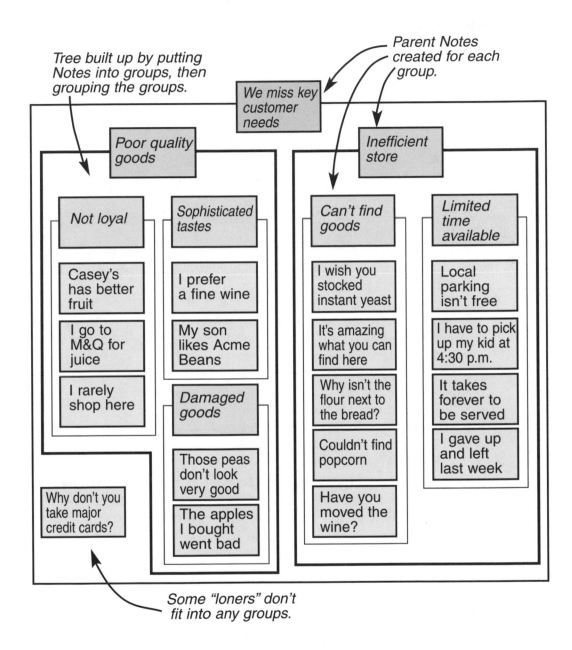

Bottom-up Tree for "Customer Comments"

How do I do it?

1. Identify objective

Identify your objective and set up the meeting as described in chapter 3. Some typical objectives are:

- Discover the real problem behind all the complaints we are receiving from the sales department.
- Find out how I see the world by grouping a large set of possible needs and wants.
- Get the whole team to work together on an action plan for new product development. The plan should include all known commitments.

When the main problem is vague, word the objective in general terms. This will "widen the net" and encourage more creative ideas to be generated. For example:

- Should we replace machines more frequently?
- Make an impact at the exhibition.
- What's bugging the printing division?

The Bottom-up Tree is primarily a method for *discovering* how a collection of individual information chunks fit together. Thus, it is less structured than the Top-down Tree. You don't need additional questions in the Help Area. Of course, you can add constraints or thought triggers if this will help achieve your objective.

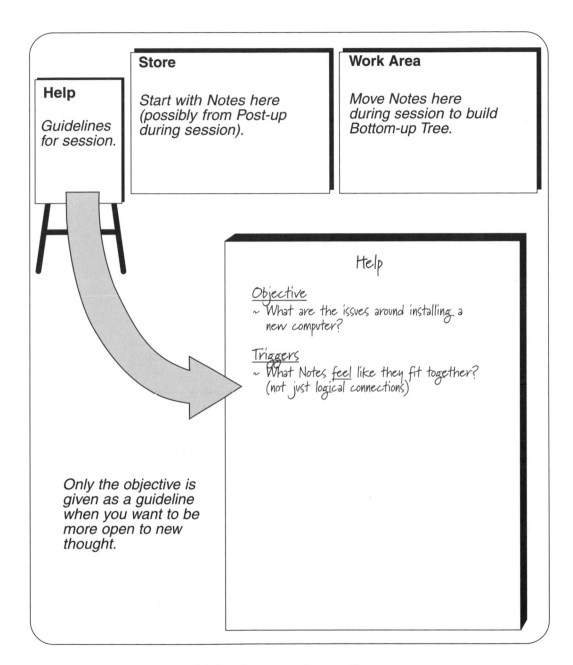

Objectives and questions

2. Collect information chunks

Use the objective from Step 1 to guide a Post-up session. Collect individual chunks of information about the problem and stick these up anywhere in the Store area.

Write each Note so it can be read and understood by itself, with only the objective to give it context. The Note may contain few words, but often it will be a complete phrase or sentence. Vague information is worth including, particularly if you are investigating an uncertain or creative situation.

Depending on the type of information you're collecting, the Post-up may be a fast session, completed in a single meeting, or a longer process, lasting days or even weeks.

3. Shuffle the Notes

When the Post-up from Step 2 is completed, shuffle the Notes in the Store area by swapping random pairs. This is done to break up patterns. People follow existing trains of thought and often put several logically related Notes close together. It's easier to see new patterns in a random layout than in one where strong patterns already exist.

4. Put columns in Work Area

Use a marker pen to divide the Work Area into columns that are a little wider than the Notes. If you are using standard flipchart paper, you'll see that each sheet divides perfectly into four columns.

Typically, you will need from six to ten columns total. If in doubt, start with a lower number and add more as necessary.

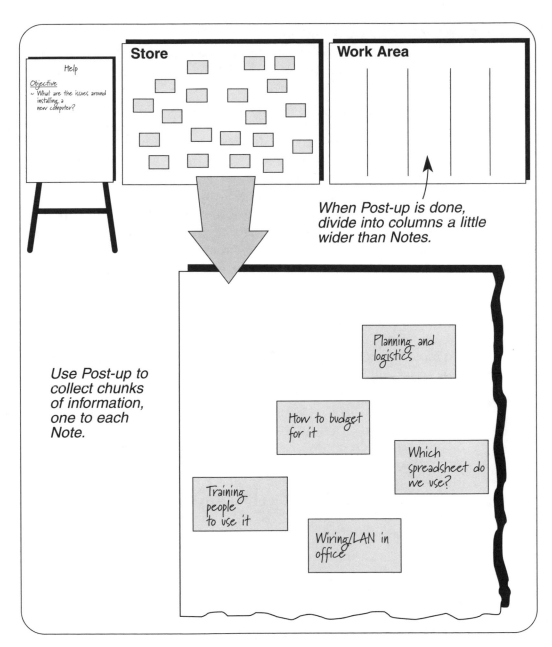

Use a Post-up to collect information

5. Move Notes into columns

Carefully read the Notes in the Store. Look for a pair that seem to be related in some way. When you find two, move them both into a single column in the Work Area.

Continue looking in the Store for pairs to start new Work Area columns or for single Notes that fit with existing Note groups in the Work Area. Move these to the appropriate column in the Work Area.

As with the Post-up, everyone does this at the same time, each working independently and silently. This may seem like a rather chaotic approach, but in practice it works remarkably well.

At first, you will probably be intent upon building your own columns. As Notes in the Store area begin to run out or there are no obvious Notes to move across, look at the columns that other people have been working on. If you can find Notes to move into their columns, do so.

A further step is to "steal" Notes from other columns. If someone moves a Note away from where you think it should be, look at the column where they moved it. Ask yourself if that is a better place for the Note. If you still think it should be where it was, move it back. This can result in silent "battle," with Notes being moved back and forth. If it looks like a stalemate, write a duplicate and add a "D" to indicate this.

If a new piece of information occurs to you as you are moving Notes, write it on a new Note and put it either in the Store or in an appropriate column.

Don't put too many Notes in one column. If more than about seven to ten appear together, look for ways of splitting them into two columns.

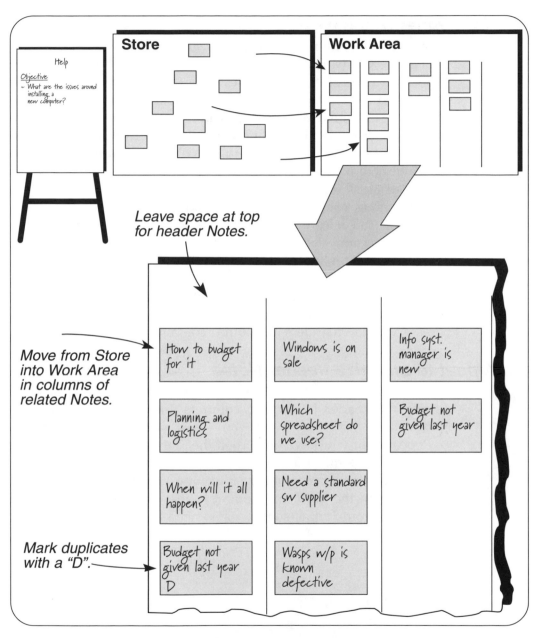

Building up the tree

6. Add header Notes to columns

Eventually the Note moving will slow and stop. Don't worry if you still have several Notes in the Store. This step will find homes for them.

Take each column in turn and discuss the Notes in it. Try to understand the common factor between them.

When you agree about the meaning of the column, write a column-header Note. Use a different color of either Note or pen to set it apart from the other Notes in the column. Stick this one at the top of the column.

This discussion is often illuminating and results in Notes being moved among columns as people realize and agree on the best groupings. You may even want to merge or split columns as the groupings become clearer.

Keep an eye on any Notes left in the Store. Try to move these to columns as headers are written and you improve your understanding of both individual columns and the main problem structure. When you are finished, no Notes should be left in the Store. If necessary, put remainders in columns containing a single Note.

7. Repeat to organize header Notes

Make a second copy of each header Note. Repeat the above process, putting the header Notes into columns and adding new header Notes.

Repeat until you have one "root" header Note that summarizes the whole problem.

Because this step is usually short, you can discuss it out loud. Depending on the problem, the root header may be directly above the headers from Step 6 (so there is no need to duplicate them).

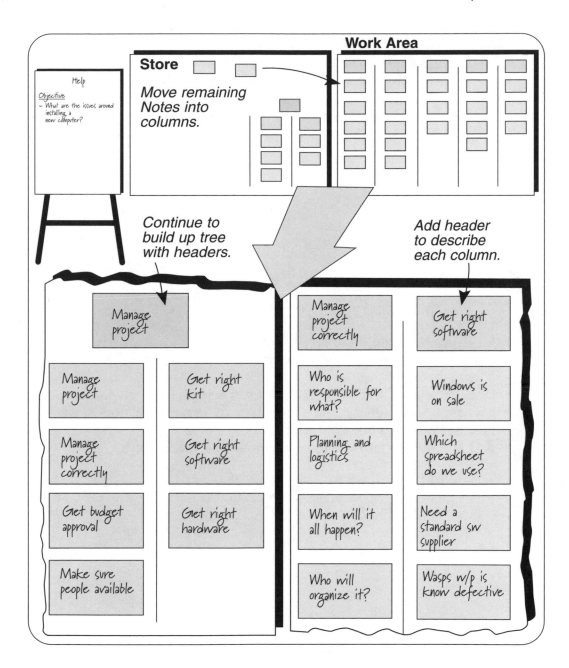

Building up the tree

8. Check completed tree

When the tree is completed, stand back and reread it. Ask questions to make sure it will help achieve the original objective.

If you were reworking a "stuck" project, did you use creative new ways to organize Notes? Or did you stay with old, familiar groupings?

When you are happy with the tree, you may want to redraw it in a different format taken from the illustration for tree layouts on page 51.

Bottom-up Tree Keys

- Use a Post-up to collect the information chunks.
- Move the Notes into columns of related items.
- Keep moving Notes between columns until you have finished sorting them.
- Discuss columns and add header Notes to summarize each column.
- Discuss how headers relate and form them into groups, adding a header Note for groups of headers.
- Add a "root" header Note to summarize top-level headers.

8 The Information Map

What is it for?

To show complex relationships between information chunks.

When do I use it?

When you know or suspect that the information chunks are related in a complex, many-to-many relationship.

It's particularly useful for nonstructured, creative sessions. For example, you can play with the results of a Post-up and rearrange the Notes to see if patterns begin to emerge.

Use it when you are investigating interrelated causes in a particularly messy problem.

Information Maps concern *understanding*. They can answer questions such as, "What is the real cause of this problem?"

Use a map instead of a tree when the relationship between information chunks is complex, rather than a simple parent-child hierarchy. You may have already tried to use a tree and failed because the relationships didn't fit the hierarchical structure. One of the benefits of using Notes is you can simply rearrange them into a Map without rewriting them.

Use the Information Map rather than an Action Map for general situations, not for planning projects or mapping processes.

How does it work?

Many problems have a messy, complex structure. Any one information chunk may be related to any number of other chunks. The Information Map will help you discover and demonstrate this picture by laying out chunks and drawing links between them.

The relationship between two information chunks often flows in one direction only. For example, freezing weather may cause ice on the road, but ice does not cause freezing weather. Use arrows to show this directed relationship.

Directed relationship

Arrows may have different meanings in different maps. In the same map, though, they usually have only one meaning, such as "causes," "belongs to" or "is near." All you need to know to start interpreting a map is what the arrow means (which should always be clearly defined).

Information Maps may not show *all* possible relationships. Sometimes the key relationships you're interested in remain hidden. To avoid this, identify relationships using a consistent approach, such as by asking a standard question. Consistency ensures that only the key arrows to help you meet your objective of using the map are shown.

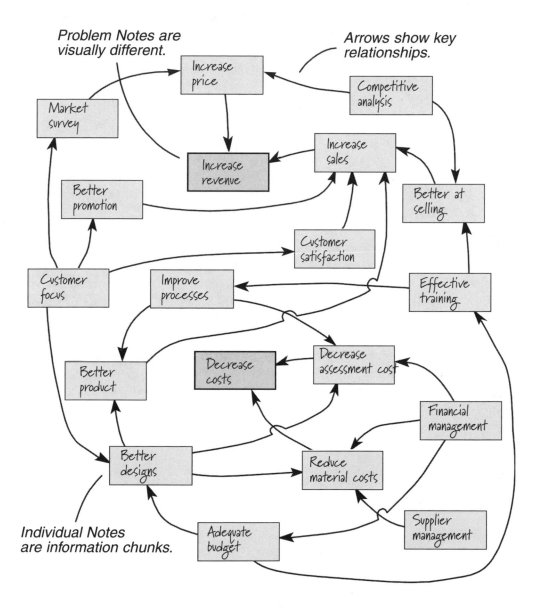

Information Map

The Information Map usually starts with one or more "problem" or *root* Notes. The Map can also have several points of interest, which may prompt important decisions. For example:

- *Chains* of Notes have one arrow between each. For example, a nail on the road causes a puncture, which causes the vehicle to swerve, which causes an accident. This direct relationship means that removing the nail at the start of the chain will also prevent the accident at the end of the chain from happening.
- *Bottlenecks* occur when many arrows flow into a single Note, but very few arrows leave it. Imagine several major roads passing through a single town, resulting in bumper-to-bumper traffic—that's a bottleneck.
- *Sources* exist when arrows only flow out of, not into, a Note. For example, a government agency provides information to various different organizations. In practice, even the government agency must get its information from somewhere. In an Information Map, sources typically lie at the edge of the problem. You're not interested in investigating beyond them.
- *Sinks* are Notes with arrows flowing only into them. For example, documents are placed into a central filing system. The root Note may well be a sink.

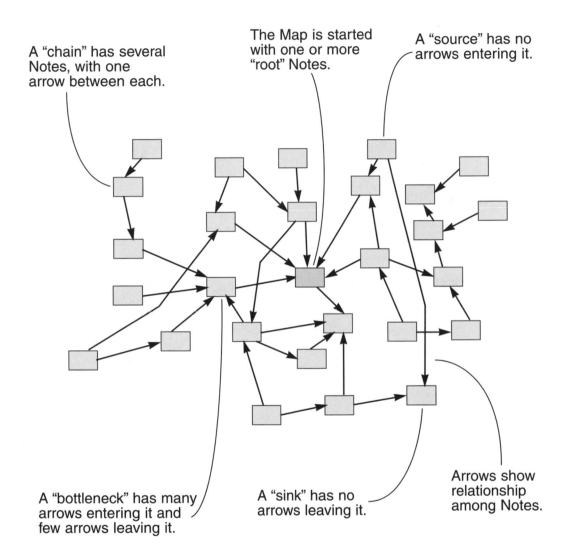

A "chain" has several Notes, with one arrow between each.

The Map is started with one or more "root" Notes.

A "source" has no arrows entering it.

A "bottleneck" has many arrows entering it and few arrows leaving it.

A "sink" has no arrows leaving it.

Arrows show relationship among Notes.

Parts of a Map

Notice the difference between the links on a tree and those on a map. On a tree, the lines group a whole family together. On a map, one line shows the relationship between only two chunks of information.

Because maps show complex relationships between Notes, the map layout is likely to be less clearly structured than a tree. As a result, maps can be more difficult to interpret. Take more care in their construction if other people will be looking at them.

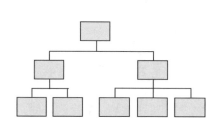

Relationships among Notes in a tree are clear from the structure.

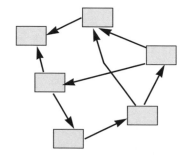

A map needs arrows to show the relationship structure.

Tree structure versus Map structure

Building the Map

How do I do it?

1. Identify objective

Identify your objective and set up the meeting as described in chapter 3. Some typical objectives are:

- Find the main causes of printer failure.
- Understand how the major roads in the area connect.
- Find the informal social network in the office.

2. Identify mapping guidelines

Use the objective to identify one direct question to ask of each Note that will help find the other Notes that are connected to it. Questions for the objectives above might be:

- What directly causes this?
- Which roads does this one connect to?
- Who knows this person socially?

The question will highlight the verb or verb phrase that describes the arrows between each Note. For example:

- causes
- connects to
- is friends with

Also identify any constraints that may be used to help select Notes and arrows more precisely; for example:

- LaserJet 4Xi only
- Interstate highways only
- Full-time employees in the finance office who have social contact with each other

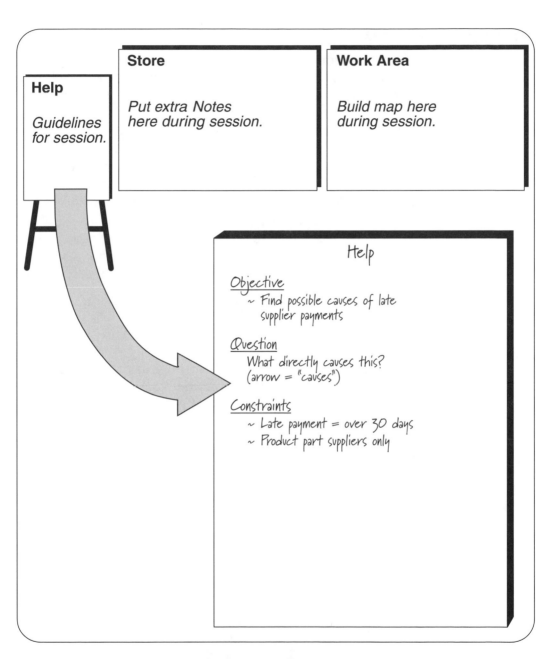

Objectives and questions

3. Identify root Note

Use the information on the Help page to write a clear and unambiguous root Note. This Note will start the map. The root may be a statement describing a problem or any other relevant information. For example, the objective "Determine factors affecting product-cost increase" may result in a root Note that says "Increase in product cost."

To make this Note stand out from the others, use a different color Note or pen.

Stick the root Note in the middle of the Work Area, so the rest of the map can be built up around it.

There may be more than one root Note. For example, when mapping out the supplier chains to a group of company divisions, there would be one Note for each "root" division. Other multiple Notes would also exist, one per supplier.

4. Identify Related Notes

Identify the direct relatives of a root Note by asking the question from Step 2. Write each related item on one Note and stick them up in the Work Area, spaced around the root problem Note.

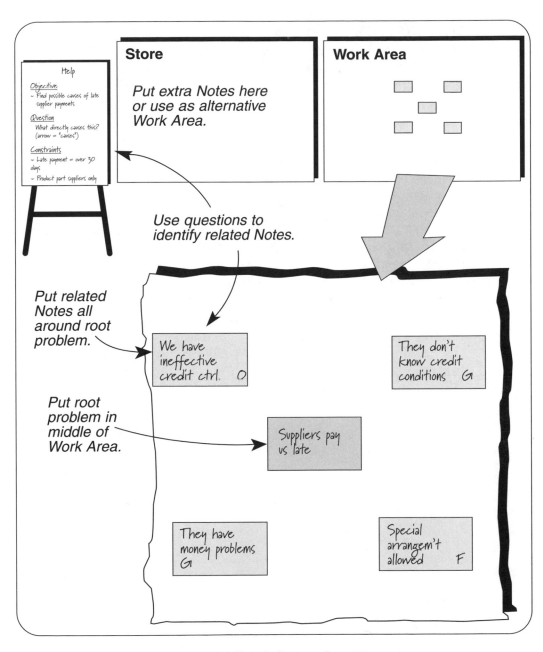

Building the Information Map

5. Repeat to find more Notes

For each Note identified in Step 4, find new related information chunks by repeating the process of asking the questions from Step 2.

Position these new Notes around the Note they relate to. If they appear to be related to other Notes, position them between their relations so it will be easier to add arrows later.

When all related chunks have been added around a Note, put a check mark on it. This will help you keep track of Notes you haven't dealt with yet. Marking completed Notes is especially useful when the diagram becomes more complex.

When sticking up Notes, leave enough space between them for arrows. When a relationship exists between two distant Notes, the connecting arrow must run around all the Notes lying between them.

If Notes become too bunched up, so that it is difficult to add new ones, rearrange them to provide more space. You can also rearrange Notes as you discover new relationships between them.

Do a Post-up beforehand as an alternative or supplement to identifying new Notes as you are building the map. The Notes may also come from a "failed" Top-down Tree, when you realize an Information Map is a more suitable tool. In either case, put the Notes in the Store and select them as required.

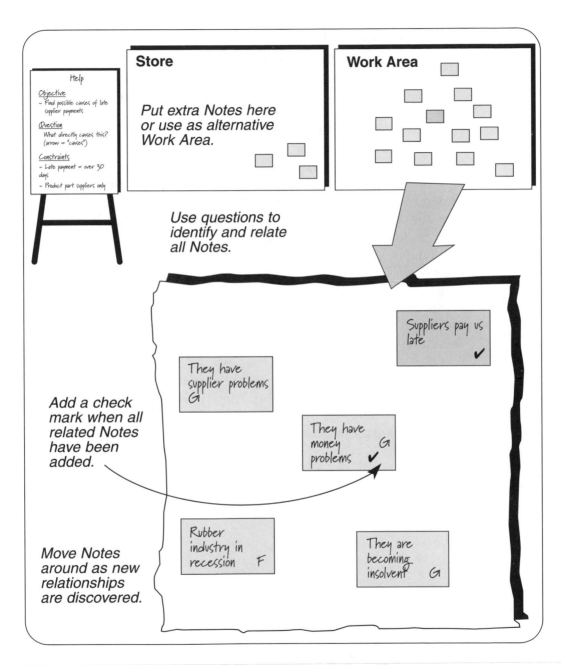

Developing the Information Map

6. Add arrows to show relationships

For each Note, ask the same questions from Step 5 to create and position the Notes, this time adding arrows to show the relationship.

As each Note is incorporated into the map, cross out the check mark that was added in Step 5.

Beware of adding too many arrows. It may become difficult to see useful information in the map. This can happen when indirect relationships are shown as well as direct ones. For example, a broken vase is directly related to it hitting a wall, but it is only indirectly related to the anger of the person throwing it.

If you discover more Note chunks to add in this step, simply slip them in. Add arrows when necessary.

If you are drawing an arrow to a distant Note and the line crosses other lines, you can prevent confusion by adding a "hump" to jump over the crossed lines.

Although the arrows should all have the same meaning (such as "causes"), some relationships may not follow these rules exactly (a variant might be, "has some kind of impact on"). These relationships are still worth noting. In these cases, use a dotted arrow to show that it doesn't have the same meaning as the other arrows. For example, in the following diagram, the known recession in the rubber industry probably has an impact on a supplier's ability to pay. It's not considered a direct cause, however.

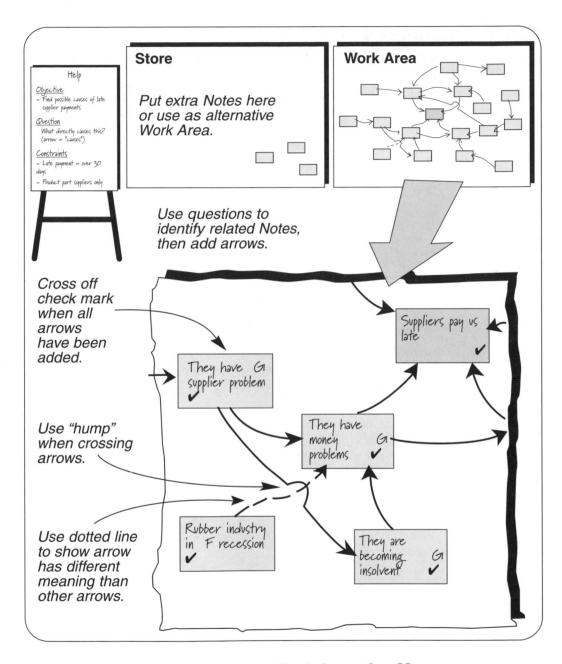

Adding arrows to the Information Map

7. Check completed map

When the Information Map is finished, check that all necessary relationships are identified and correctly shown with arrows.

If you are uncertain about the relationships or the completeness of the information in the map, leave it alone for a while. Come back to it from time to time to see if you want to change any of it.

When you are happy that the map is complete, use it for its intended purpose, such as identifying a key cause for further action.

Information Map Keys

- Define questions to help you identify Notes and relationships.
- Place one or more root-problem Notes centrally.
- Identify related Notes by repeatedly asking the same defined question.
- Put related Notes near each other.
- Add arrows to show relationships.

---

9 The Action Map

What is it for?

To show how a set of actions are related.

When do I use it?

An Action Map is concerned with *doing*. It answers questions such as, "What do we have to do first?" Use this tool when you are mapping any set of tasks or actions to show how they depend on each other; for example, to show that one task must be completed before another may start.

Use it to understand the logical sequence of tasks. Ask "What *could* I do next?" Often, after a task is completed, you'll be able to identify several more that could be done at the same time or in any chosen order.

Use an Action Map to plot the sequence of tasks. Ask "What *will* I do next?" to make firm decisions about what to do when. It can be a good idea to find the logical order first, then rearrange the tasks into the actual order in which you will do them.

You can use it to map out work processes, either as they exist or as you expect them to be performed. The map may then become a part of work-standards documentation.

It is valuable for planning projects. Use a Top-down Tree to break up the problem into individual tasks, then use an Action Map to organize their sequence.

How does it work?

A common problem with any set of actions is to decide what must be done and in what order. From the big picture of how a company operates down to production-line assembly, work processes need to be understood, designed, communicated and followed. Action Maps are designed to solve this group of problems. Basically, the Action Map is a detailed form of the more general Information Map.

The Notes in an Action Map usually represent specific actions. These actions may range from broad functions, such as "sell products," to more specific acts, such as "choose cereal" or "insert screw." The arrows usually indicate sequence, meaning "is followed by."

Each Note in most Action Maps reflects approximately the same degree of activity. You would not expect to find "build rocket" and "insert screw" on the same map. Multiple levels of action can be *nested* — a single Note on one map is expanded into an entire map at the next level down. In this fashion, you can map the activities of an entire organization.

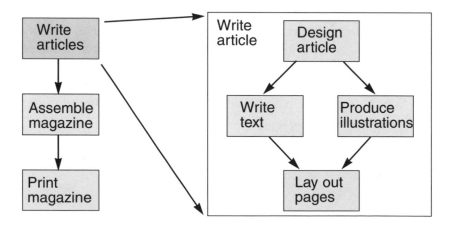

Nesting Action Maps

Action Maps often start at one point and finish at another. These points may be shown by Notes with "Start" and "End" written on them. Progress towards completion tends to be indicated by most arrows pointing in the general direction of the end point.

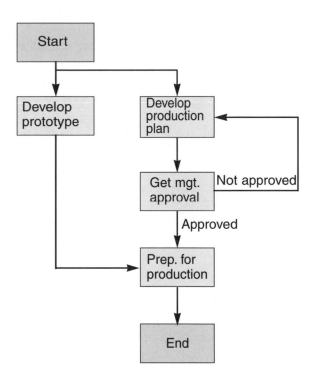

Action Map

How do I do it?

1. Identify objective

Identify your objective and set up the meeting as described in chapter 3.

There are usually two levels of objective in Action Maps. The first level relates to use of the overall plan or process map. For example:

- Redesign key business processes to align with our stated market strategy.
- Reduce assembly time of XM30 engine.
- Bring new dress designs to the market.

The second level helps give further direction when building the map. For example:

- Identify key business processes and how they interrelate.
- Map current assembly process of XM30 engine.
- Build plan for market promotion, showing tasks and how they depend on each other.

2. Identify constraints

Add constraints that must be considered. Often these focus on time, cost (including equipment and people) and quality. They may also indicate the level of detail required. For example:

- Must fit on a single page and be easily understood
- Include each movement of part or person
- Each task should be performed by one person with less than 20 hours of effort.

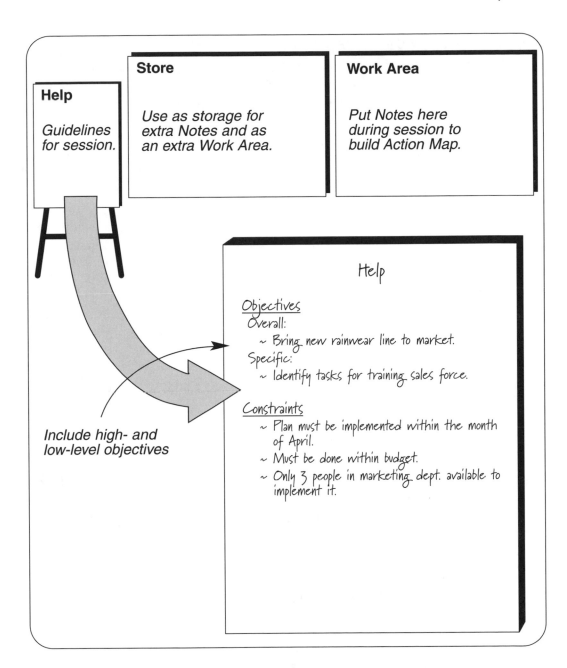

Objectives and constraints for Action Map

3. Identify expected map shape

Decide the shape of the map based on the type of information you are laying out. This will reduce the number of times Notes have to be reorganized to make more room. For example:

- Show a single person's process as a simple sequence of actions set out in the same order as they are performed. Use separate branches to show alternative sets of actions after a decision is made. These maps are often long and narrow, so start from the top of the Work Area and build the map downward.
- When mapping a high-level process, use arrows to show the movement of items or information between sub-processes. This gives a broad diagram that may flow in several directions at once. The best shape is left to right or outwards from the middle (starting with the key processes).
- Build a plan by using arrows only to show what *must* follow what. This kind of diagram tends to be wide and is best laid out from left to right.

Begin the map with a "Start" Note to make it easier to read the flow from the beginning.

4. Map out what happens first

The initial action Notes simply ask "What must happen first?" Place them after the start to show they are independent of one another. For example, when building the map from left to right, put them one above the other, well-spaced, so Notes can be added later.

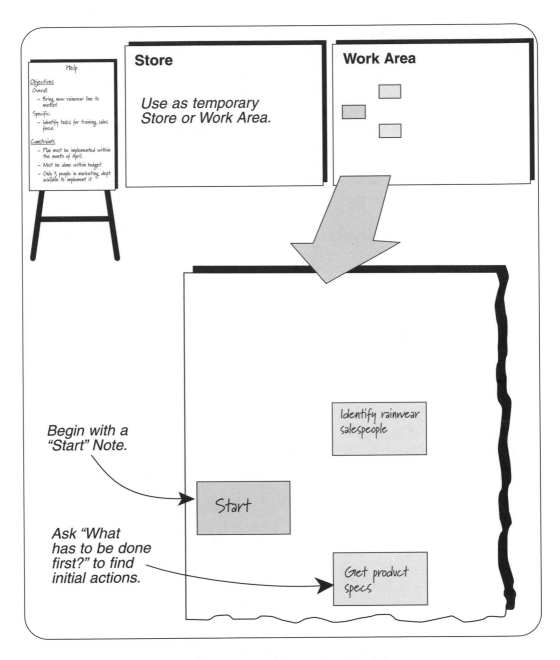

Starting to build the Action Map

5. Add subsequent actions

Continue to build the map by asking of each Note added, "What immediately follows this?" Then write a Note that answers the question. Place it so it's clear that it follows the previous action.

Often it will become apparent that an action should be done earlier or later. When this happens, rearrange the Notes to reflect that.

Sometimes a Note action follows more than one other Note. For example, say that two actions produce items that are all used in the action that follows. In this case, position the follow-up Note between the two and to the right of them both.

Some actions are not easily identified by asking, "What happens next?" In these cases, try an alternative strategy:

- Do a Post-up first to identify tasks to choose from when building the map. You may have to move Notes around a lot and combine Notes that are too detailed. Still, it's a useful method for creative or uncertain situations.
- Use a Top-down Tree to break down the problem, then use the bottom-level leaves as actions in the map. This is works particularly well for building plans.
- Start in the middle with well-known actions and work outward, asking what must be done before and after each Note. Or start at the end and work backward.

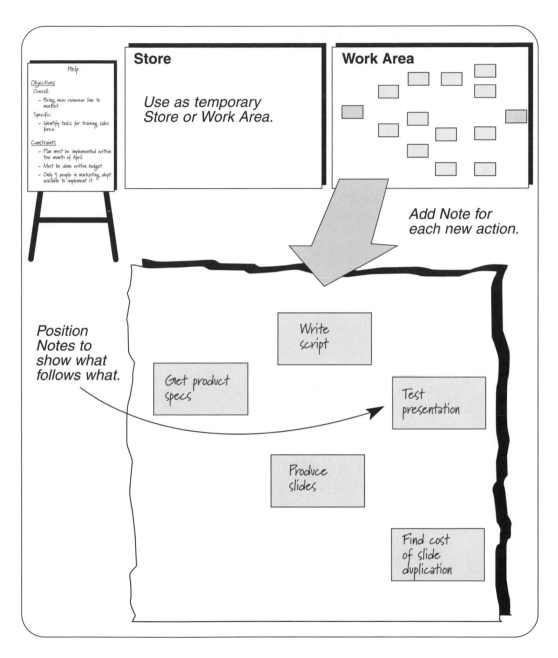

Building up the tree

6. Add arrows to show sequence

When the Map is complete, add an "End" Note. Place it just past the last Note. Start and end Notes help to contain the map, clearly showing it as one process or plan.

Go back through the map again, adding arrows to show the sequence of actions. If arrows cross one another, use a "hump" to show they do not join together.

Avoid adding arrows while generating Notes in earlier steps. Although it can be helpful to show unclear sequences, Notes often are moved when new actions or sequences are identified.

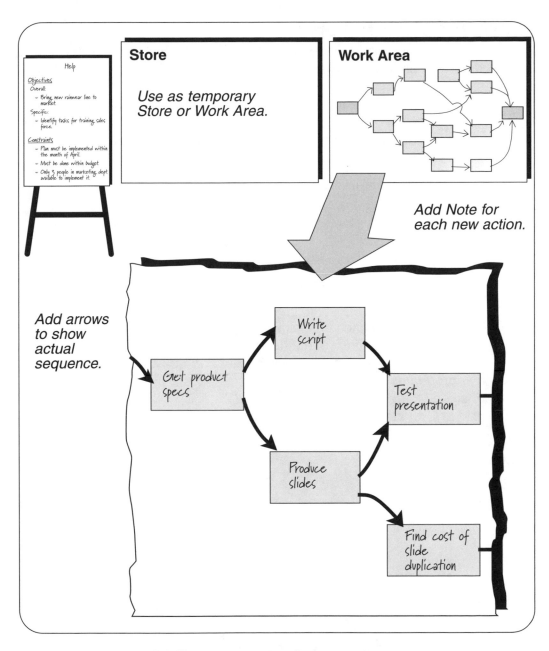

Adding arrows to show sequence

7. Check completed map

When the Action Map is complete, check that the objectives and constraints can be met.

It's not uncommon to produce several small Action Maps, nested together as on page 90, rather than one large one. In this case, the next step may be to select one Note from the completed map and expand it to a new, lower-level Action Map.

Action Map Keys

- Define objectives and constraints.
- Find actions by asking, "What happens next?"
- Keep actions about the same complexity and quality. Use nesting if appropriate.
- Position Notes in sequential order.
- Add arrows at end to show sequence.

Part III
Putting the Post-it® Note Tools to Work

The Post-it® Note Tools are for use in real problem-solving. You need an organized approach to make them work well, which this part of the book supplies. When you are familiar with the tools and approaches, you can start to improvise, combining tools and thinking up new ways to use them.

Putting the Post-it® Note Tools to work

10 Solving problems

The following lines, by Rudyard Kipling, contain the passwords of problem-solvers everywhere:

I keep six honest serving men
(They taught me all I knew);
Their names are What and Why and When
And How and Where and Who.

The simplest way to take Kipling's advice is to adopt a general questioning approach to problems. When faced with an uncertain situation, ask: "What is important? Why should it be fixed? What and where are the facts?" and so on. It's amazing how much you can achieve with an open mind and a refusal to take everything at face value.

The questioning approach, although useful, can still leave you unsure about where to start and what to do next. Asking questions may help, but if you ask the wrong questions for the current place, time and person, you might get confused.

To avoid this, organize yourself so you approach a problem with a reasonable degree of confidence. One way is to use a rigid set of rules that dictate every step. This may work for some problems, but it can be too inflexible in many other situations.

An alternative is to use more flexible guidelines you can change to fit the problem at hand. This framework provides the foundation of the problem-solving method. It enables you to define the more detailed actions within each stage.

Generally, the size and complexity of the framework will reflect the size and importance of the problem. It makes sense to spend time and effort to solve serious and costly problems. Smaller, everyday problems, however, need a more lightweight approach.

You can use one of three frameworks:

1. For everyday problems, take a general *questioning approach* and use the Post-it® Note tool that seems most applicable.

2. For more challenging problems, use the *simple framework* described on the opposite page. Use Post-it® Note tools individually or in combination to help solve the problem.

3. For serious problems that require more organization, assemble a team of people who can work together to solve the problem. Use the *project framework* described starting on page 106.

A simple framework

When faced with any problem, begin by asking these few basic questions:

1. *What am I trying to achieve?* If you can describe where you're trying to go, you're more likely to get there.

2. *What is the real problem?* Select the best tool to organize and understand the information around the problem. Use a Post-up to gather information. Organize it with a Tree for simple situations or a Map for more complicated ones. Look for the important things to fix. If they're not clear, use a Swap Sort.

3. *What is the solution?* Use the results to obtain a better understanding of the problem and then find an appropriate solution. Do a Post-up to find possible solutions and a Swap Sort to find the best one.

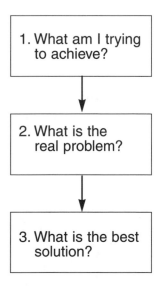

A simple framework

A project framework

Difficult and important problems need a more formal approach than those problems addressed by questioning or the simple framework on the previous page.

The framework described here is built on just three of Kipling's questions: "What?" "Why?" and "How?" Within the framework, of course, many more questions may be asked.

The project framework takes steps to find the *cause* of the problem before trying to find a suitable solution. This approach makes sure you treat the real problem, not just the symptoms.

The project framework seeks not only to fix the problem but also to ensure it stays fixed. At best, it enables you to learn from the experience so that future problems are easier to solve.

The main steps to follow are:

1. **What** is the problem?
2. **Why** is it happening?
3. **How** can you fix it?
4. **FIX IT!**
5. **Why** did it work or not work?
6. **What** next?

The following sections expand on each of these steps and suggest which tools may be used in conjunction with them.

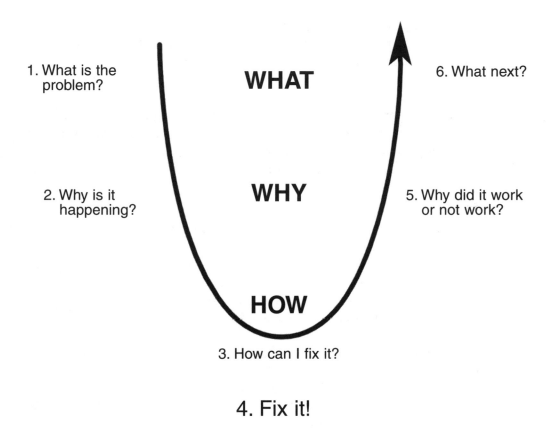

1. What is the problem?

6. What next?

2. Why is it happening?

5. Why did it work or not work?

3. How can I fix it?

4. Fix it!

The project framework

1. What is the problem?

Defining the problem is often a messy stage. You know you are hurting, but don't really know what's wrong. The first task is to create problem statements and goal statements to help you focus your efforts. They will also help you to tell later if the problem has been fixed.

Spend some time on this stage. It can take a lot of effort to gather the facts about a problem. If you're in a hurry, you may want to skip through it more quickly, but be prepared to recognize this in Step 5 (Why did it work or not work?).

Why are we here?

First, create a brief *problem statement*, outlining the basic problem and why you need to fix it now.

When possible, include facts and figures and indicate why this problem is more urgent than others. For example, "Deliveries have been consistently late over the past six months, resulting in about 50 complaints from major customers. Several customers are threatening to move to the competition." This statement paints the big picture, which gives urgency and direction to all future actions.

- Use a Post-up to help gather information about the problem.
- Organize the results of the Post-up in a Bottom-up Tree to help find the problem statement.
- Or, instead of a tree, use an Information Map to connect the results of the Post-up.

What are we trying to achieve?

Create a *goal statement*, or ultimate objective, that describes what the situation will look like when you have solved the immediate problem.

You can have multiple goal statements, but they may complicate the solution if you try to solve everything at once. In fact, it's usually safer to fix things one piece at a time. Big changes require big efforts and can fail in many different ways.

Aim to base your goal on facts, rather than opinions. Take time to measure things such as current customer-complaint levels, along with other factors, such as how severe the complaints are.

A good goal statement helps you identify when the problem is fixed. It should introduce some kind of constant measurement. For example: "Within the next six months, reduce customer complaints about Keydo products to fewer than three per month."

- Draw an Action Map of the process being fixed to clarify what happens and to identify measurement points.
- Use a Swap Sort to choose the best measurement.
- Do a Post-up of possible goals. Use the problem statement and Action Map you already generated to help focus this effort. For example, identify problem areas to be fixed. To decrease defects by half in the future, you have to know what the defects are now.
- Use a Swap Sort to choose the best goal.
- Do an Action Map to plan the rest of the project, including the people needed and the tasks to be completed.

2. Why is it happening?

When you know what your problem is, the next step is to find out why it's happening.

Have you ever tried answering a small child who keeps asking you, "But *why*?" By about the fifth "why," if you're still answering, your answers are probably quite detailed. The Japanese recognize this with a saying: "Ask why five times."

Beware of skipping this stage. It's a common trap to leap from problem to solution without considering whether you're fixing the cause or just treating symptoms.

- Do a Top-down Tree (asking "Why?") to find out what is causing the problem.
- Or, instead of a tree, use an Information Map to map complex "cause" relationships.
- Use a Swap Sort to determine the most important causes to fix. As with goals, don't try to fix too many causes at one time.

Ask "Why?" five times

3. How Can I Fix It?

After you've defined your problem and identified its causes, move on to finding solutions. Consider a number of alternative solutions and narrow them down to a few you will act on.

When selecting solutions, make sure that you are able to fully implement them. The simplest way is to find actions for which you do not need authorization and where you do not have to persuade other people to implement the solution.

Beware of finding fault with other people. Conflict will arise and nothing will get done.

If other people are affected by your solution, take time to organize your information. Be prepared to negotiate and persuade. They might have to give you permission or resources to enable you to implement your solution. You may want them to do something for you—possibly even permanently change what they do.

- Do a Post-up of potential solutions.
- Use a Top-down Tree, starting with the cause from Step 2. Ask "How?" to find the detail of how the problem can be fixed.
- Use a Swap Sort to select the best solution.

4. Fix it!

In this stage, you act on the solution identified in Step 3.

At first, it may seem simple to put into effect the solution you're sure will fix the problem. Beware—many projects stumble at this stage. Theories must become practices and commitments must become actions.

If other people are involved in implementing the solution, make sure they receive adequate training. What they should do may be clear to you, but it must be *crystal clear* to them.

It can also be tempting at this stage to make last-minute changes, using different solutions that suddenly seem better. If you're tempted to take this path, be prepared to face the consequences in Step 5. If the wonderful new solution doesn't work, you'll have to answer why.

• Do an Action Map of the steps to take in implementing the solution. Include actions that make sure people understand any changes that affect them. Also plan to measure the changes in some way so you can tell whether the solution has worked.

5. Why did it work or not work?

After implementing the solution to the problem, stand back and watch. With luck, it'll work as planned, but the best-laid plans do not always work as expected. It's important to treat the solution as if it's "on trial" until it has proved itself.

If the solution didn't work as planned, look at how the process failed, *not* who's to blame.

The most important part of this stage is to *learn* about both the problem and the overall problem-solving process. Write these lessons down so you clarify your own thoughts and can pass this learning (instead of blame!) to others.

- Do a Post-up and Bottom-up Tree to identify reasons for success or failure. Ask: "Why did it happen as it did? What were the key reasons?"
- Do an Action Map of actual events. Then compare the results with the plan from Step 3. Ask: "What unexpected events occurred? What was not planned? What unnecessary actions were planned?"

6. What next?

What you do next depends on what happened before. You can take three possible actions:

1. *If the solution did not work,* go back to a previous step to find a solution that will work. For example, if Step 5 showed that the cause from Step 2 was not that critical after all, then go back to Step 2 and find a *real* cause to fix. When a solution didn't work because in practice it was unworkable, go back to Step 3.

2. *If the solution did work,* go back to a previous step to make further improvements. Review Step 2 to fix another cause. Or go back to Step 1 to find a new problem to fix or to refine the goal in order to fix a new part of the problem.

3. *Whether the solution worked or not,* close down the project. The problem should now be fixed. Or perhaps it turned out to be not worth the effort to solve. The subsequent action may be to celebrate, to disband or to start another project. If the solution didn't work, the new project may be similar to the first.

- Do a Swap Sort of possible subsequent actions.
- Do an Action Map to plan the next steps.

11 Post-it® Note Tools in Action

Post-it® Note tools have now been explained in detail. Suggestions have been given for using them in structured problem-solving situations. This chapter presents a more complete example of how they can be used in practice.

The situation described below involves a number of the Note tools, showing how they can be used to help solve actual problems.

The problem

Gilbert Rogers, the Technology Services manager, stared with concern at a piece of paper. The memo from Rebecca Hughes, the Operations Manager, was only one of a steady stream of complaints he'd been receiving about his department and the services they provided for the company. He sighed, put the paper down and rubbed his forehead, wondering what to do next.

By the next departmental meeting, Gilbert had decided what action to take. As he described the problem and his proposals to his co-workers, he was glad to see they took the situation seriously. When they started discussing it, however, they disagreed about the true nature of the problem. When it was time to take a break, no progress had been made.

Step 1: What is the problem?

As they all sipped coffee, Gilbert stood up and explained what they needed to do. It was the team's problem and they had to work together to solve it. They would use a project framework to find the problem and make sure it was properly fixed. Within this framework, they would use Notes to capture and understand the pieces of the problem.

The first step was to discover the fundamental problem. To help collect their thoughts, Gilbert decided to use a Post-up. They would start this in the meeting and then leave it up for a week. People could add facts, opinions and ideas as they thought of them.

In the meeting, they identified 25 Note thoughts. Another 10 were added during the week. The Help page and final Post-Up follow.

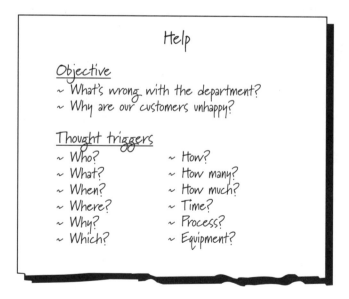

Help page for Post-Up to find problem

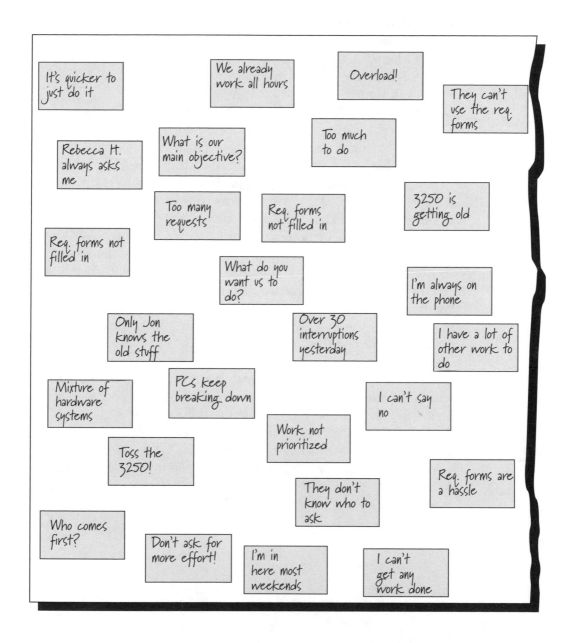

Posting up information chunks about the problem

At the end of the week, they sat and looked at the problem. After a period of silence, Greg Streeter, a junior analyst, pointed out what everyone else was already thinking: He still didn't understand the basic problem. Sure, there were many valid points there, but what did they add up to?

Gilbert nodded slowly as the others murmured their agreement.

"You're right, Greg," he said, as he taped a couple of pieces of flipchart paper together to make a new Work Area. "And I think a Bottom-up Tree will help us make sense of this. The Help page can stay the same, but there are a few new rules for you to learn."

Before long, the only sound was the rustle of paper and scratching of heads. They gradually moved the Notes into columns of related issues. Silent battles raged as individuals moved Notes back and forth between columns. Finally, a peace was found as people either agreed or made duplicates. Some new Notes were also added as the structure of the problem gradually dawned.

Adding header Notes was surprisingly easy because everyone soon agreed on the meaning of each column. This final agreement also allowed the last few "orphan" Notes to find a home in one of the existing columns.

Gilbert added a couple of Notes above the headers and linked them to the headers with lines. This divided internal problems from external problems, those felt outside the department.

As a summary, they agreed on a problem statement as follows:

We are working hard, trying to keep up with requests from our customers. But we've become so driven by interruptions that we've lost sight of what we're trying to achieve.

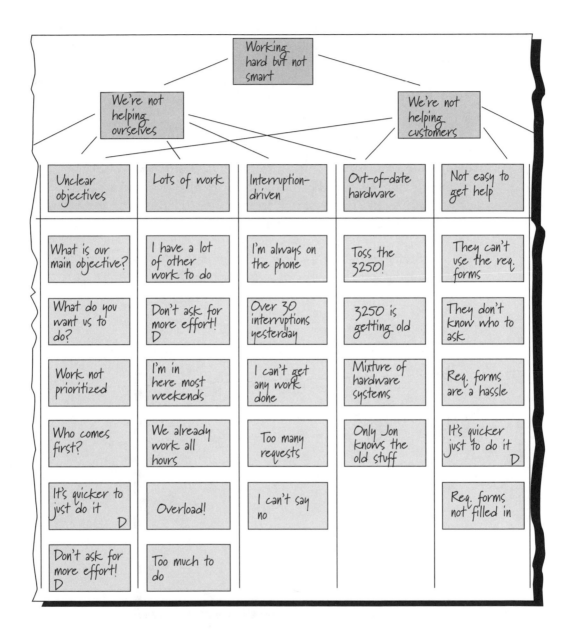

Bottom-up Tree to find basic problem

Now that the main problems were identified, several people had ideas for fixing them. They wanted to implement their solutions right away.

"Hold on, folks!" called Gilbert, smiling at their enthusiasm. "We want to be sure we're fixing the right thing before we rush into action. Let's use a Swap Sort to help."

When writing the Help page, there was some discussion over the priority of different criteria. Gilbert was certain that customer problems were more important than their internal, departmental problems.

Using the criteria, the problems from the Bottom-up Tree were easily sorted into order of importance.

From this, they created a goal statement:

> *Our customers can get help in a way that helps us to help them, resulting in their increased satisfaction with our service.*

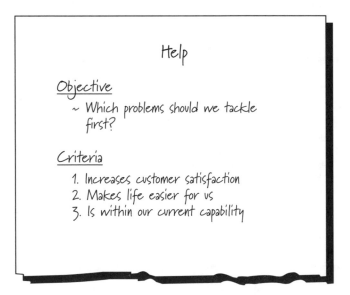

Help page for Swap Sort to find key problem to fix

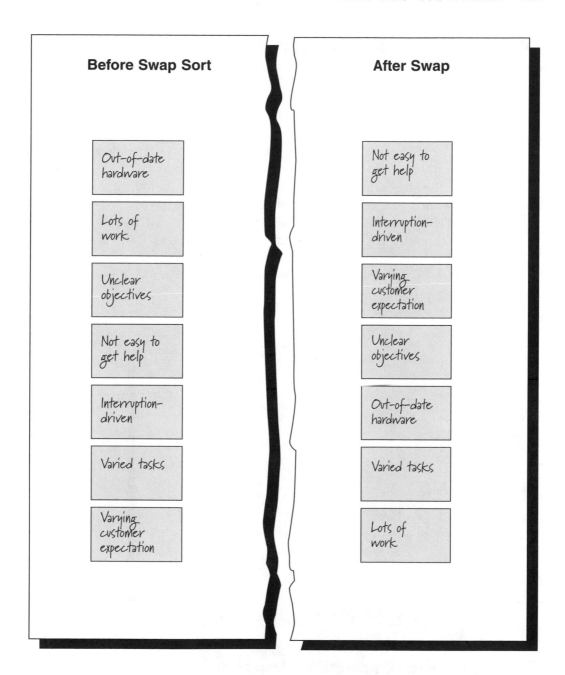

Before Swap Sort

Out-of-date hardware

Lots of work

Unclear objectives

Not easy to get help

Interruption-driven

Varied tasks

Varying customer expectation

After Swap

Not easy to get help

Interruption-driven

Varying customer expectation

Unclear objectives

Out-of-date hardware

Varied tasks

Lots of work

Swap Sort to find key problem to fix

Step 2: Why is it happening?

"OK," said Gilbert, looking around at his team. "We now know where we stand and where we want to go. The next step is to find out why it's happening."

Immediately, everyone had a number of suggestions. Most of them were ideas to fix the problem, rather than its causes. Thankful for the structure the project framework gave, Gilbert got everyone's attention and explained what they would do next.

They decided to tackle the top two problems. This allowed them to consider both the external, customer concern and the internal, departmental problems. Because these two problems seemed to be connected, Gilbert decided to use an Information Map to understand their relationship and find the key causes.

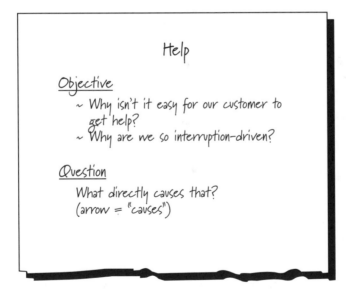

Help page for Information Map to find problem causes

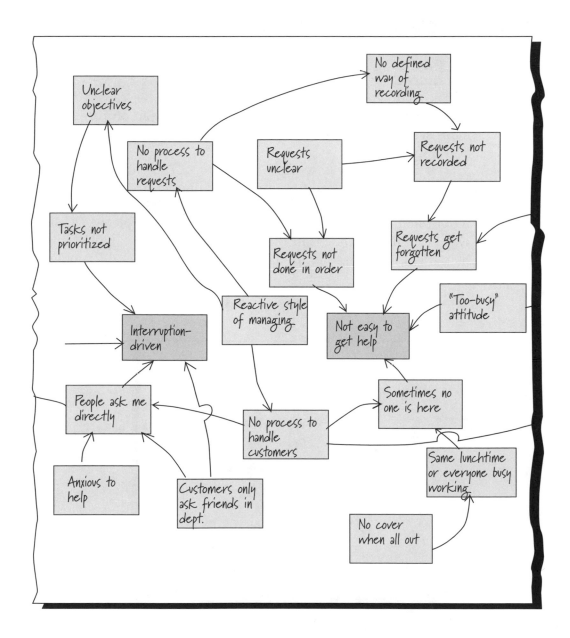

Information Map to find problem causes

Step 3: How can we fix it?

"Of course!"

They all agreed the Information Map made the causes of their problem much clearer to see. Their focus had been on running the main systems. They weren't recognizing that requests for help were also important.

The next step was to find a solution. The Information Map revealed a pressing need for a process to handle customer requests.

"Before building the process description, I think a Top-down Tree would help us identify the tasks that must be completed." Gilbert was becoming confident in the power of the Post-it® Note tools to help them work together to rapidly solve each part of the problem.

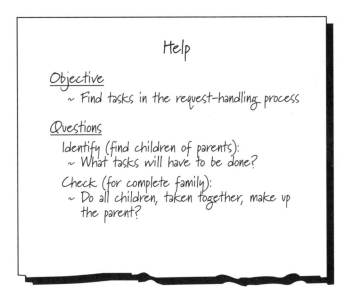

Help page for Top-down Tree of tasks

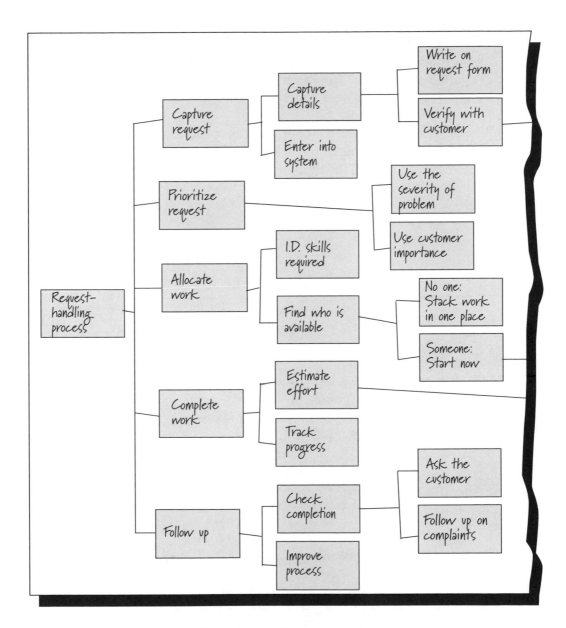

Top-down Tree of tasks

As a technology group, they were familiar with techniques for charting processes. Several of them were eager to use a detailed method of designing the request-handling process. Gilbert, however, pulled them back. He pointed out that an Action Map was just as good and would be a much quicker way of piecing together the steps of the process.

Once they started mapping the process, even the doubters became enthusiastic as the solution quickly took shape.

Later they used the map of the final process to help persuade and train other people affected by the process, including their customers.

Help

Objective

~ Overall: To efficiently and effectively satisfy customers' needs for help.

~ Specifically: To define process to handle customer requests.

Constraints

~ No extra people available

~ Some of existing budget may be available.

Help page for Action Map of request-handling process

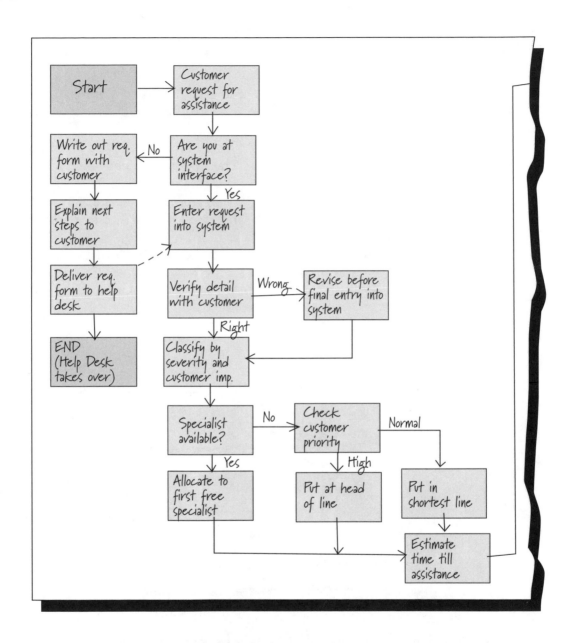

Action Map of request-handling process

Step 4: Fix it!

"That was surprisingly quick!" remarked Selena Vasquez, the response-team leader. "From confused to action in just over a week. It must be a record!"

Gilbert smiled. "There's one last thing to do before we put it into action—confirm who's doing what. The Action Map has helped, but I want to make sure all the responsibilities are understood."

He then drew some columns on the dry-erase board and took out the Notes. Several people smiled. They knew this would be another quick and effective session.

Gilbert explained that he wanted to check that all of the high-level tasks were accounted for. He was now comfortable enough with the main Post-it® Note tools to try his own variation, based on the Post-up.

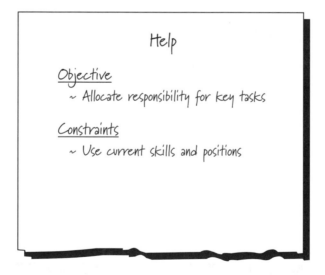

Help page for modified Post-up to check responsibilities

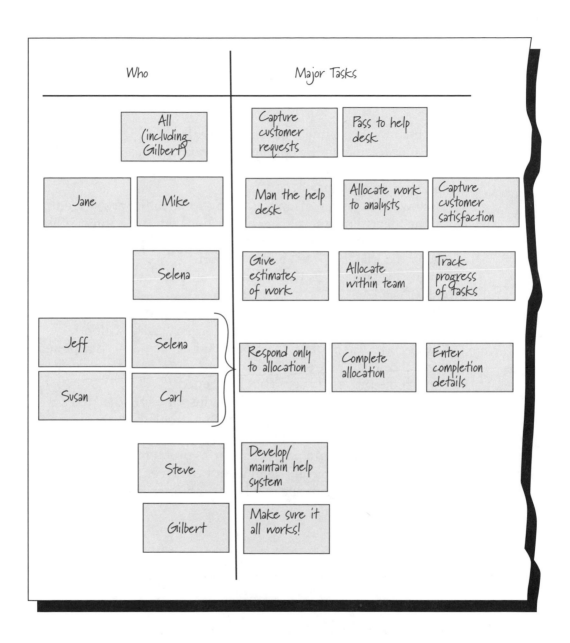

Modified Post-up to allocate responsibilities

Step 5: Why did it work or not work?

At the end of the first month of operation, the team sat down together to discuss how well the process was working in the "real world."

For the most part, it was successful, with some glowing feedback on the improvements. In particular, several financial analysts had praised their responsiveness to problems in the salary-administration system.

They were, however, disappointed by some rather angry feedback from the development manager. He had put in a high-priority request for assistance but hadn't received any help for three days.

"Why did this happen?" asked Gilbert.

"Well, I've checked. The request was put into the system on Monday," said Mike.

"But I didn't get it until Thursday," Susan said.

"Then why did it get stuck in the process?" asked Gilbert.

"Let's use the Notes to model what actually happened," suggested Selena. "If we make one Note represent one request, we can watch the process to see what happened."

Gilbert agreed, pleased that suggestions for using the Notes were now coming from the team. Soon the problem was clear—the finance problem had also come in as high priority and had been put ahead of the development manager's problems. Because both problems were for Susan, she didn't receive the development manager's problem until she'd solved both finance problems.

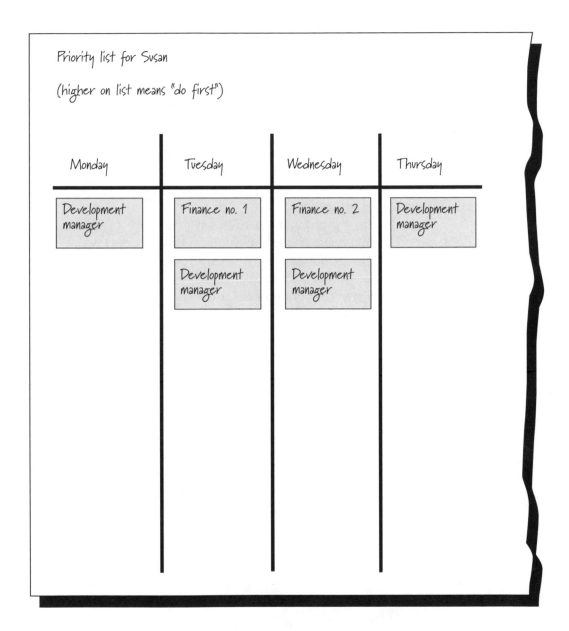

Priority list for Susan

(higher on list means "do first")

Monday	Tuesday	Wednesday	Thursday
Development manager	Finance no. 1	Finance no. 2	Development manager
	Development manager	Development manager	

Using Notes to model the request line

Step 6: What next?

The next step was now clear. The process needed correction to prevent some high-priority requests from being pushed down the list by other high-priority requests. They found a solution by adjusting the Action Map and the corresponding system controls.

Then they went back to Step 4 to check the system again. They followed each step carefully, making sure the changed process worked as planned. Also, they recognized new problems and found and eliminated their causes.

In the following months, they found a few more problems and determined their causes. Then they changed the process to cope with them. Post-it® Notes continued to be useful tools for finding the problems. All six tools were used at one time or another.

In the review meeting six months after they had started, Gilbert showed them a graph of the customer satisfaction they had been measuring. It showed how satisfaction had risen and was now steady at an all-time high.

As the project ended, they concluded that the framework and tools had provided just the right amount of guidance without being too limiting. In the later stages, their increasing familiarity with the principles of the Post-it® Note tools had enabled them to use variations of the basic tools, shaping their use to the specific need of each step.

12 Advanced Usage

When you've been using the tools for a while and are comfortable with how they work, you could continue using them as described in the previous chapters. You could use these methods in whatever form works well for you.

On the other hand, you could start pushing the boundaries. You could constantly look for new ways of making better and more effective use of Post-it® Notes in your own problem-solving.

This chapter looks at some of the other ways that Notes can be used, including the following:

- Extending or changing the rules for existing tools to make them easier to use or to solve a specific problem.
- Combining existing tools so they work in harmony to solve a single problem.
- Inventing completely new tools to use in your particular work environment.

These examples can be used as described or as an inspiration for you to find your own way of using Post-it® Notes in rapid problem-solving.

Extending the standard tools

To extend the standard tools, first examine and understand the basic rules. Then examine and understand the problem you wish to solve. The next step is to change the rules and try it out.

Accelerated Swap Sort

In the standard Swap Sort, Notes are first placed randomly in a vertical list. You can speed the Sort by putting the Notes that you think are more important near the top of the list. If you are correct, this will result in fewer swaps, which is particularly useful if you have a long list.

A second way of accelerating the Swap Sort is to compare and swap *any* pair of Notes. Thus, if a Note at the bottom of the list looks important, you can compare and swap it with the top Note.

Nothing is free. The price you pay in both of these variations is that you make fewer comparisons. Because of this, you reduce the chance of making breakthrough discoveries when a Note you initially thought was unimportant actually turns out to be valuable.

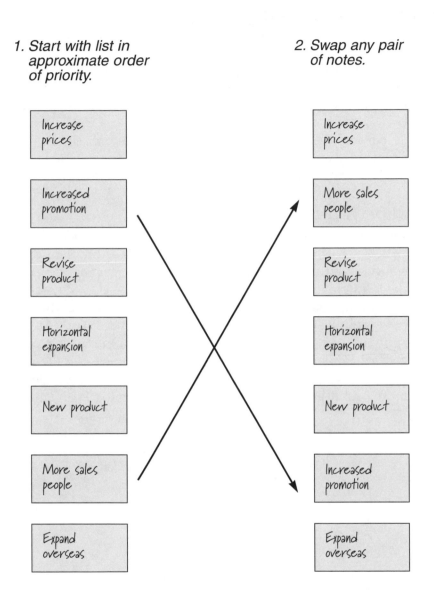

Accelerated Swap Sort

The Inside-out Tree

You can start a Top-down Tree in the middle and work both ways. If you go down the tree by asking, "How?" you go up even further by asking, "Why?" You can then find alternative solutions by going back down a different branch.

For example, if a person asks for a promotion, ask "Why?" to find she wants recognition. Then ask "How?" to discover a high-visibility project that's an acceptable alternative.

Investigation Top-down Tree

When using a Top-down Tree, you can vary the question asked at each level. This way you go from the original problem down to its solution and risk management in a single tree. See the example on the following page.

When using Top-down Trees to go down a number of levels, however, you do tend to run out of space in the Work Area.

If you can focus on specific Notes as you build the tree, you can control the space problem. Use the principles of divergence and convergence to develop only relevant branches or those that look more promising than the others (see pages 6 to 9).

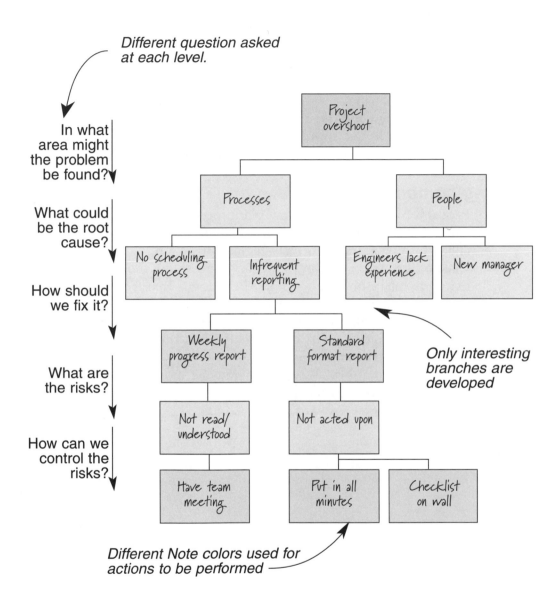

Investigation Top-down Tree

Combining tools

Tools are great when used alone. But they can be particularly powerful when used in combination, especially when the Notes from using one tool are simply transferred to use on another tool.

The simplest and most common form of combining tools is using Post-up results as input in other tools. This principle can be extended for specific situations, as in the following examples.

Planning combinations

Post-it® Notes are ideal for planning, an activity that's often confusing. Too often complex, all-encompassing plans turn into chaos when you try to turn strategies into action.

The illustration on the opposite page shows how a high-level objective can be broken down in a Top-down Tree. The bottom-level leaves should be actionable tasks. Usually, these will be delegated to individuals. Ideally, you'll be able to keep track of their progress. (Hint: If you track activity on a weekly basis, then most tasks should take about one week).

These bottom-level leaves can now be moved directly into an Action Map. As well as saving time, this method makes sure all actions are carried forward.

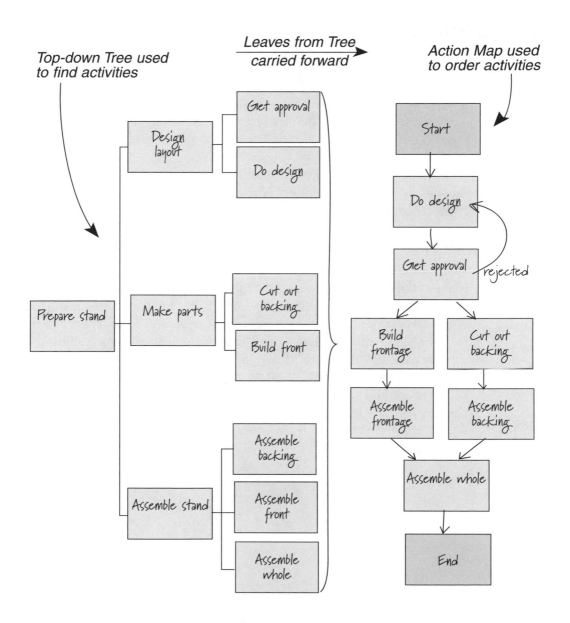

Planning combinations

The Sorted Tree

When doing either a Top-down Tree or (especially) a Bottom-up Tree, you can end up with large families of Notes at the bottom of the Tree. Although the families are large, all members are not necessarily equal. For example, potential solutions to a problem may vary in importance.

This situation can be addressed by using a Swap Sort. Sort the leaves within their families, without having to move them away from their parent.

The Naked Tree

Trees can appear naked in winter because they lose all of their leaves. This idea can be translated into a way of combining the Top-down Tree and the Post-up to structure creative sessions. This combination can direct the session so you solve your problem faster.

As shown in the illustration, first do a Top-down Tree of the whole problem. Break it down into the various subject areas in which you can be creative. Follow this with a short Post-up for each of the identified subject areas. Put the Notes in a column underneath the appropriate leaf of the Tree.

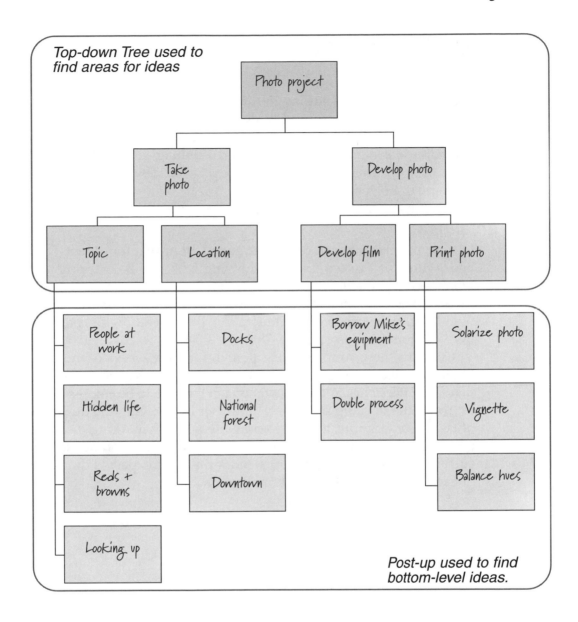

Top-down Tree used to find areas for ideas

Photo project

Take photo

Develop photo

Topic

Location

Develop film

Print photo

People at work

Docks

Borrow Mike's equipment

Solarize photo

Hidden life

National forest

Double process

Vignette

Reds + browns

Downtown

Balance hues

Looking up

Post-up used to find bottom-level ideas.

Naked Tree: Combining Top-down Tree and Post-up

Developing new tools

The principles of capturing information chunks on Notes and organizing them can be used to develop completely new tools. As you become more experienced and comfortable with using and extending the standard tools, you start thinking in a Post-it® Note kind of way. This leads to the discovery of new tools to solve individual problems.

Task timelines

During planning, Notes can be extended from the Top-down Tree and Action Map into a diagram showing who will be carrying out what action and when it will be completed.

As with any innovation, borrow ideas from existing tools whenever appropriate. The illustration on the following page is derived from the classic Gantt Chart.

Columns show your reporting period, typically weeks or months. Rows show the people who will be working on the tasks. The tasks are placed as milestones in the week in which they are to be completed.

You could develop this diagram further by showing the duration of tasks. For example, add a second Note per task marking the start point. Other variables associated with planning can also be added, such as the effort involved, the calendar time, the expected duration of each task, unscheduled tasks and so on.

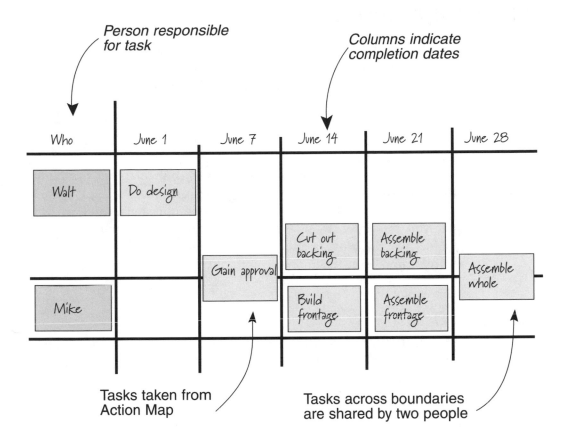

Person responsible
for task

Columns indicate
completion dates

Who	June 1	June 7	June 14	June 21	June 28
Walt	Do design				
			Cut out backing	Assemble backing	
		Gain approval			Assemble whole
Mike			Build frontage	Assemble frontage	

Tasks taken from
Action Map

Tasks across boundaries
are shared by two people

Developing new tool: Task timelines

Bottom-up Sets

In some problems, the relationships between various chunks are complex enough to use an Information Map, but not certain enough to add arrows between Notes.

The tool required for this type of situation is somewhere between the grouping of the Bottom-up Tree and the complex structuring of the Information Map.

The answer isn't simply to add arrows, but to move the Notes (after or during a Post-up) into overlapping groups of related chunks.

When you have done this, and if the boundary between groups is clear, you can draw circles around them, forming overlapping sets.

A set, by the way, is another name for a nonordered list. They become interesting when they overlap with one another.

Top-down Sets

Sets, like trees, can be built top-down as well as bottom-up. When you know what the groupings are going to be, define the sets first, drawing and naming overlapping circles. Then use a Post-up to fill in the sets and overlaps, as in the illustration.

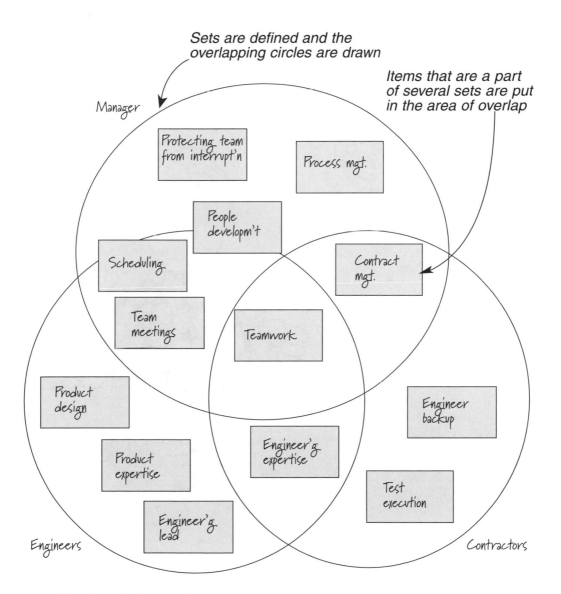

Sets are defined and the overlapping circles are drawn

Items that are a part of several sets are put in the area of overlap

Manager

Protecting team from interrupt'n

Process mgt.

People developm't

Scheduling

Contract mgt.

Team meetings

Teamwork

Product design

Engineer backup

Product expertise

Engineer's expertise

Test execution

Engineer's lead

Engineers

Contractors

Objective: Identify contribution to success of team members

Top-down Set

Advanced Usage?

Appendix: Practical Tips

Whenever you use tools of any kind, there are always tricks of the trade. These help make the job quicker and easier. They help you perform tasks that would otherwise seem almost impossible. Professionals tend to acquire these skills through a combination of sitting at the feet of their teachers and from their own long experience.

This appendix does not aim to make you an instant expert, but a few helpful pointers may ease some of the difficulties you experience early on.

On first using the tools . . .

The first time you use the tools, expect to be hesitant and uncertain. Expect to feel a little awkward. But also recognize that you're in a learning situation. You will improve with practice. Let your problems become interesting opportunities to find out how the tools work.

A good way to learn is in collaboration with other people. Sharing the experience will help all of you grasp the practical principles of each tool more quickly than you would if you were working alone. The tools described in this book work particularly well when used with a group, although you can also use them when working alone.

On peeling Post-it® Notes . . .

Post-it® Notes come in pads of about 100 Notes. When you peel them off backward, the top part of the Note, where the adhesive is on the back, curls. When you post them up on the wall, they tend to stick out at an awkward angle, rather than lie flat. They also have the tendency to fall off, especially if you're moving them around and haven't pressed hard to make them stick well.

A simple solution is to pull the Notes off *diagonally forward and slightly up,* not backward. For example, see the illustration on the following page. This technique may seem awkward at first, but you'll have a flatter, more usable Note.

Another solution is to buy packs of Pop-up® Notes, which are deliberately stuck together in alternate directions to solve just this curling problem. These are best used in the special holders available for them. The Notes can then be easily pulled out one at a time, much like tissues from a box.

Pop-up® Notes

Wrong: Ripped off backward
Note curls and doesn't stick well

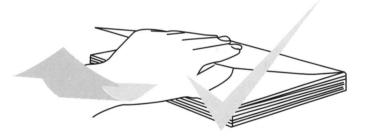

Right: Pull forward diagonally and slightly up, toward you
Pulls off Note with minimum curl

Pulling off Post-it® Note for minimum curl

On different-sized Notes . . .

Post-it® Notes come in several different sizes. Two sizes are most useful in problem-solving.

The most popular size, 3 x 5 inches, is useful for working in groups. Notes are stuck to a vertical surface and everyone can see them from a distance. To make them more readable, use a marker or felt-tip pen.

Smaller-sized, 1-1/2 x 2-inch Notes are useful when you're working alone or in a small group. In this case, you can write on the Note in ordinary handwriting with a pen or pencil.

On different Note colors . . .

As discussed in previous chapters, you can use more than the standard yellow Post-it® Notes. Use red, blue and yellow for the FOG factors (Facts, Opinions, Guesses) when doing Post-ups. Use red, blue and green for successive levels of header Notes in the Bottom-up Tree. Use a red root Note in the Information Map.

These are not the only times you can use different Note colors. For example, when changing the question in the Top-down Tree, also change the color of the Note.

If you don't have more than one color Note, you can achieve a similar effect by using different pen colors. Or you can mark the Notes in some way—with broad colored borders, for example.

This can be read from across the room.

Use large Notes for groups, with large writing so you can read it from a distance when it's stuck on a wall.

This can be read only when you are close to it.

Use small Notes when working by yourself, or in small groups, so you can fit more in the Work Area.

Use the right size Post-it® Note

On working surfaces . . .

Notes don't stick to every surface. They work best on a dry, smooth surface, such as a dry-erase board or a window. Perhaps the best surface is paper (after all, their original use was as a bookmark). They don't work on rough or dirty surfaces. If in doubt, test them by sticking a Note to the surface and blowing hard to see if you can dislodge it.

Dry-erase boards are useful for working with tools such as the Top-down Tree or either of the Maps. You will probably want to draw and redraw lines between the Notes. The problem here, as with other large flat surfaces like walls and windows, is that you can't take them away. If you wish to take a copy of your final diagram with you, you'll have to copy it to a more transportable piece of paper.

Flipcharts enable you to take away or move around a group of Notes, but they may be too small to contain a complete diagram. Compromise by taping several flipchart pages together to make a larger working area. You may also use a large sheet of poster paper. Completed diagrams can then be transferred to the walls in your office.

When working with small Notes (1-1/2 x 2 inches), use a blank page in your notebook. You can leave them there for reference, or build the diagram gradually, as you walk from place to place.

3M makes a couple of additional products that can be used for working surfaces.

Post-it® Meeting Charts are a cross between flipcharts and Post-it® Notes. They have a broad strip of the special glue across the top of the back. This lets you stick them to walls quickly and easily without having to use tape or tacks.

Post-it® Easel Roll is similar, but comes on a roll and has the adhesive on two edges, allowing a wide Store or Work Area to be firmly stuck to the wall.

On making the tools work for you . . .

When you first use the Post-up or Action Map or any of the other tools, follow the guidelines given in this book. They give a consistent approach that is easy to learn, use and share.

But if you find that the tools described here don't fit your way of working, don't be a slave to them. Once you're comfortable with and understand the practical principles, feel free to bend and change the rules, as suggested by the examples in chapter 12. Invent new uses or combine tools for new situations. You can even use the tools themselves for this task!

When changing the way you use the tools, involve the people you'll be using them with. If they're changed to suit just you, then you'll lose the great benefits of using them in groups.

INDEX

Page numbers in **bold type** denote diagrams.